PENGUIN BOOKS

BEYOND 2020

A.P.J. Abdul Kalam (1931–2015) was one of India's most distinguished scientists, responsible for the development of the country's first satellite launch vehicle and the operationalization of strategic missiles. He also pioneered India Vision 2020, a road map for transforming the country. The President of India between 2002 and 2007, Dr Kalam was awarded honorary doctorates from thirty-eight universities and the country's three highest civilian honours—the Padma Bhushan (1981), Padma Vibhushan (1990) and Bharat Ratna (1997). A prolific and best-selling author, he conducted lectures on societal development in many international institutes and was involved in research on different societal missions.

Yagnaswami Sundara Rajan is a well-recognized authority and a thought leader on technology development and business management. He held various positions of responsibility related to science and technology across industries and shaped several key policies. Currently an honorary distinguished professor at ISRO, Bengaluru, he was awarded the Padma Shri in 2012.

A.P.J. ABDUL KALAM AND Y.S. RAJAN

BEYOND 2020

2020

A Vision for Tomorrow's India

PENGUIN BOOKS

An imprint of Penguin Random House

PENGUIN BOOKS

USA | Canada | UK | Ireland | Australia
New Zealand | India | South Africa | China | Singapore

Penguin Books is part of the Penguin Random House group of companies
whose addresses can be found at global.penguinrandomhouse.com

Published by Penguin Random House India Pvt. Ltd
4th Floor, Capital Tower 1, MG Road,
Gurugram 122 002, Haryana, India

Penguin
Random House
India

First published in Viking by Penguin Books India 2014
Published in Penguin Books 2016

10 9 8 7 6 5 4 3

ISBN 9780143426066

Typeset in Bembo Std. by Eleven Arts, Delhi
Printed at Manipal Technologies Limited, India

MIX
Paper | Supporting
responsible forestry
FSC® C043100

Contents

Contents

Let us recall a profound statement made by Maharishi Patanjali some 2500 years ago:

> When you are inspired by some great purpose, some extraordinary project, all your thoughts break their bounds. Your mind transcends limitations, your consciousness expands in every direction, and you find yourself in a new, great and wonderful world. Dormant forces, faculties and talents come alive, and you discover yourself to be a greater person by far than you ever dreamt yourself to be.

Why don't our present and future leaders, irrespective of which party they belong to, our scientific community, our industrial leadership and our farmers and administrators, and above all our 600 million–strong youth, look every day at this wonderful message that a great saint left for India and the world?

If every citizen of the nation says 'I can do it!' that will result in all of us saying 'We can do it!' and lead finally to 'The nation will do it!'

Introduction by
A.P.J. Abdul Kalam

Our book *Beyond 2020* has fifteen chapters with extensive details on how to take the nation from progress to progress by pushing through missions on industries, services and agriculture. I feel the crying need in our country is not a shortage of plans, but arriving at the correct methodologies to implement the plans and figuring out how to reach the benefits to the people for whom the plans are intended.

Today, the challenge before India and in fact every nation is reaching the reforms and benefits to the targeted population. Based on my work with universities in India and abroad during my teaching and research association, I have come to the conclusion that it is essential to evolve a sustainable development system framework, in the way the Providing Urban Amenities in Rural Areas (PURA) project has taken root in India. The major research and action needed is on how the benefits of sustainable development can reach the targeted population of our country. Hence, we have evolved two unique systems: one is called the 'User Community Pyramid' and the other the 'Societal Development Radar'.

The User Community Pyramid (UCP) is an integrated solution based on technologies and applications for sustainable development with possible users at the bottom of the pyramid. You have to ask yourself, what sort of research you can focus on in the areas of water, energy, waste, pollution, mobility and biodiversity, and how it is going to be connected with the user community. The second system, the Societal Development Radar (SDR), reviews and monitors how the user community has benefited from the UCP. I will describe both systems based on my own experience which generated a book *Target 3 Billion*,[1] and subsequent feedback.

User Community Pyramid

Sustainable development refers to a mode of human development in which resource use aims to meet human needs while preserving the environment so that these needs can be met not only in the present, but also for generations to come. The world has so far seen rapid development in the social, economic and political spheres. But due to dwindling natural resources and a burgeoning population (currently more than 7 billion in the world), today it is essential to think of sustainable development in every aspect of human life and in every sector of the economy. I often ask myself, what do we learn from the many terrestrial and mobile networks, satellites for remote sensing and communication, the many ground sensors, flight systems and all the data received from various data capturing systems? When we analyse the data, what is the resultant benefit that can be given to the rural population of 3 billion people worldwide to empower them with information, knowledge and wisdom to improve their quality of life? The UCP uses the convergence of technologies to bring development to the people using natural resources optimally for the generations to come.

My visualization of the UCP structure links the following:

1. Natural Resources
2. Information and Communication
3. Convergence of Technologies

4. Societal Business Model
5. Applications
6. Users

Now let us discuss in detail how sustainable development can be achieved in a given User Community Pyramid. There are many national initiatives at work on the ground with the help of technologies to protect the environment and bring about sustainable development, for instance:

- Sustainability for safe drinking water and water for irrigation
- Reducing pollution using technology and best practices
- Adopting more renewable energy resources to reduce dependency on fossil fuels
- Managing mobile resources so that they do not affect the environment and lead to further deterioration of health and environment
- Enrich biodiversity, thereby bringing peace and economic prosperity to the nation.

The objective of the UCP is to focus these initiatives towards the lasting benefit of the user community.

The components of the UCP are as follows:

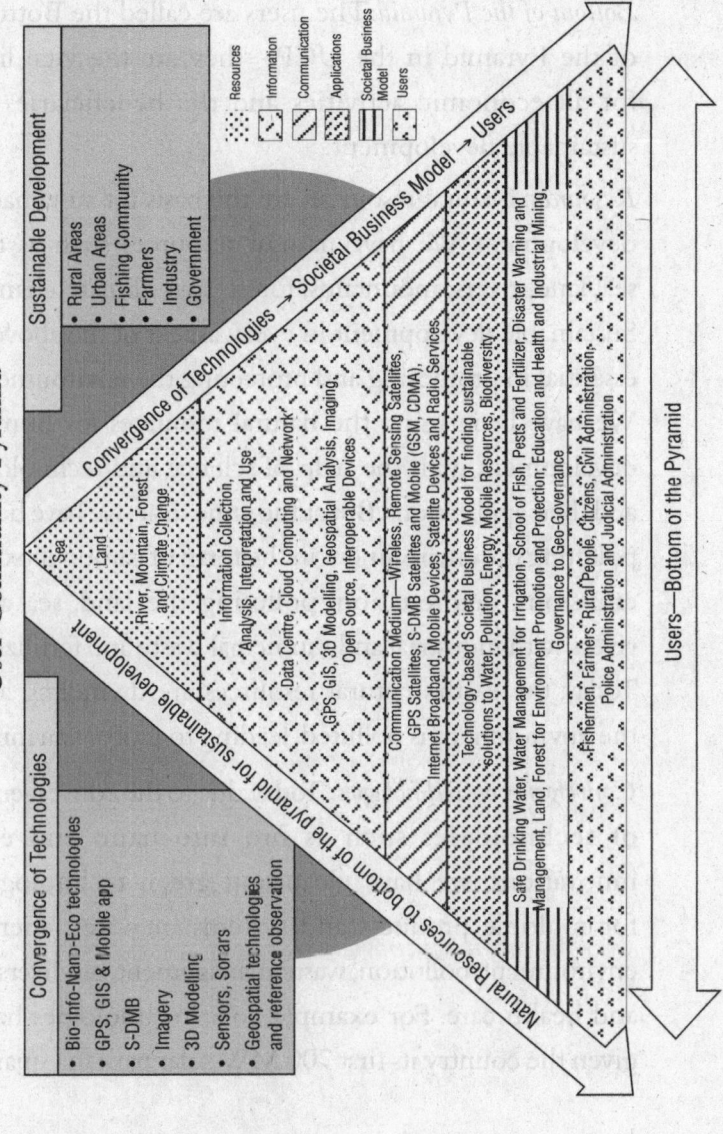

Bottom of the Pyramid: The users are called the Bottom of the Pyramid in the UCP—they are the vital link for all economic activities and the beneficiaries of sustainable development.

Resources: Natural resources are the basis for sustainable development. We have natural resources such as the sea, land, rivers, mountains, forests and climate change. Sustainable development in every aspect of the above is essential in promoting and protecting the environment. We have been using the natural resources for human development with the help of science and technology and their applications. But at the same time, we have been polluting the environment in the form of carbon dioxide emissions, deforestation, polluting the land, sea and rivers with industrial and municipal waste and fertilizers. Today, the earth's natural resources are dwindling and the environment is polluted, leading to global warming.

Convergence of Technologies: Today, due to the convergence of technologies such as bio-info-nano and eco innovations, we have clean and green technologies for multiple products and systems in water, energy, environment, pollution, waste management, biodiversity and health care. For example, solar technologies have given the country its first 700 MW solar park in Gujarat;

nano-filter technology has given us safe drinking water solutions; nano-packaging and eco technologies have given us biodegradable packaging solutions. Research and development is progressing using the convergence of technologies which will give more clean and green products to humanity. Now we have to ensure that these technologies reach the user community using information and communications technologies and by evolving a societal business model.

Information and Communication: Information collection, generation and dissemination through communication networks and its technologies over terrestrial and satellite networking has attained new dimensions due to the convergence of geospatial technologies. This helps in monitoring and tracking the natural resources, and planning to improve the environment and enrich biodiversity. The mined information and its analysis transform into knowledge. Information and communications systems collect data from land and space through the terrestrial network and wireless technologies. The GIS (geographic information system), GPS (Global Positioning System) and geospatial technologies using satellite networks may acquire and analyse the data from remote-sensing satellites, including resource mapping of the land, water and seas. Modern geospatial analytical tools may analyse the wealth of data generated which may enrich the knowledge on how to bring sustainable development in multiple areas such as waste, pollution, energy, mobility and biodiversity. Using the information and communications technologies, we need to evolve an innovative societal business model so that the research results of the convergence of technologies are used for human development in a sustainable way.

Societal Business Model: At one end, technology-based systems develop out of scientific research; at the other, we need to evolve an innovative business model which will take the technologies to the users for creating sustainable development systems. We are looking at socio-economic applications from the unique societal business model which will empower and enrich users such as farmers, fishermen, skilled workers and people living in rural areas. When the sustainable development societal business model is applied, that will result in the use of available natural resources optimally, recycling them without polluting the environment and at the same time make them available for generations to come so that global peace and prosperity is assured.

Ultimately, the research results will have to benefit the people with a pollution-free green environment, safe drinking water and also water resource management. Zero-waste discharge systems will not pollute the environment, using technologies which will reduce the carbon footprint. Use of renewable energy resources for achieving energy independence and the application of navigational and resource mapping to maximize the use of mobile resources, such as river flows for the optimal utilization of water, will ultimately improve biodiversity by enriching the environment which is congenial for its growth and managing the life-cycle balance. The sustainable technologies have to help to improve the quality of living conditions of the people using the existing natural resources sustainably for the generations to come, without any depletion of the resources, using clean and green technologies. Then it is possible for the sustainable development to reach the Bottom of the Pyramid which is the ultimate benefit of the defined User Community Pyramid.

Societal Development Radar

The purpose of establishing the Societal Development Radar is to review and monitor how the User

Community Pyramid has benefited the users. Our approach on the development radar is based on eight essential empowerment attributes which are critical to the realization of our goal: a happy, prosperous and peaceful society beginning at the base of the pyramid. These traits are:

1. Access to food and nutrition
2. Access to water, both potable and for irrigation, and sanitation
3. Access to health care
4. Access to income generation
5. Access to education and capacity building
6. Access to quality power and communication applications
7. Avoidance of societal conflict
8. Access to financial services

In the SDR, we have given three targets, as shown on the radar. One indicates the current status of the eight social attributes. The second is the medium-term target. The third is a long-term target with a specific schedule. When developing technologies that are societal transformers, we can chart in advance which applications will empower the UCP, and the outcomes may be tracked and monitored through the SDR.

Development Societal Radar
Essential Empowerment Attributes

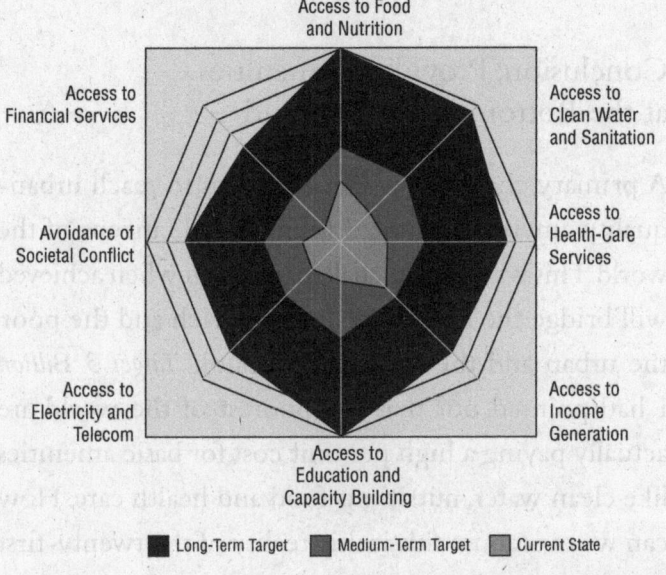

With these tools, the scientific and technological community has to refocus on how technology should be used in the twenty-first century when solving problems that are sometimes reminiscent of perhaps the nineteenth or twentieth century. We need to rethink how the convergence of technologies at our disposal can solve some of the problems of the 3 billion–strong rural population of the world and help them unleash their potential, thereby leading to a better human life across the globe, without damaging the environment around us.

Conclusion: Providing Amenities at the Bottom of the Pyramid

A primary challenge we face today is to reach urban-quality amenities to the 3 billion rural citizens of the world. This is an urgent challenge which when achieved will bridge the divide between the rich and the poor, the urban and the rural. In the book *Target 3 Billion* I had pointed out that the poorest of the world are actually paying a high per unit cost for basic amenities like clean water, nutritious food and health care. How can we overcome this ironic reality of the twenty-first century?

There are three possible methods of action that Indian societal transformers can work towards:

1. Helping identify the state of potable water availability in the region. The parameters of both overground and underground water supplies, pollution status, waterborne disease patterns and usage data should be included. This can be the basis for evolving the potable water grid.

2. Helping identify 'hotspots' for local energy generation capacity. This can include energy from waste, energy from biofuels that can be grown in wastelands, small-scale hydro plants, and so on, which can empower the local communities. This can be the basis for the local energy grid.

3. The technologies designed for sustainable development of rural areas should have the power to enhance the employment potential of the rural population.

Our book *Beyond 2020* discusses possible ways for India to become a globally competitive land with an economically developed status, and for us to reach the next stage of prosperity, where we will be counted along with the eight developed countries of the world.

CHAPTER 1

India @ 2014

A Great Achievement That Went Unnoticed

The 27th of March 2014 was a great day for Indian society. Sadly, it was a day that went virtually unnoticed. It was a day that should have been celebrated all over India because the achievement it marked was due to decades of hard work, from the topmost levels of government right down to the administrative bodies in every village, town and city; non-governmental organizations (NGOs) had channelized their activist energies in a positive direction towards this one goal, and every family had made it possible by participating in the landmark project—to eradicate polio from India.

Both of us have seen the scourge of polio first-hand. It crippled many Indians, making them dependent on others for their entire lives. Many children lost their childhood: they had to, with pain in their hearts, crawl clumsily on the floor or limp along with a stick as support, while other children ran about and played.

Thanks to the concerted work by several organizations and individuals for many decades, India is now free of polio. It was on 27 March 2014 that the World Health Organization (WHO) made the announcement. There are still a number of countries in the world where polio has not been eradicated. Some of these countries are our neighbours. The Government of India has made it a condition that Indians who visit these countries have to take a polio vaccine in advance before their visits, just as Indians have to vaccinate themselves against yellow fever before they visit certain countries of the world.

It is a great achievement for a country as large as India to have successfully eradicated polio, but to maintain a polio-free status is an equally challenging task. India had become smallpox-free, along with the rest of the world, in 1980. Many other communicable diseases in the country are now under control; leprosy is almost gone.

Why Was There No Celebration?

There have been many achievements in public health care in India. But we do not quite feel like celebrating them, because middle-class Indians—who count in the hundreds of millions now—have many pressing problems in their day-to-day lives: inflation, job insecurity, rising health-care costs, a whole set of hassles in schooling their children, and so on. And they are rightly enraged by reports of mega scams, although these are sometimes highly exaggerated for sensational value.

For those who are knowledgeable about the indicators of the well-being of people, several other statistics come up to immediately dampen the great feeling of achievement that should have accompanied the news of our becoming polio-free. In the same India, in the year 2014, some 1.5 million children will die of diarrhoea—a disease that can be easily prevented by improving sanitation conditions, providing better habitats for children and families, and giving them access to clean drinking water. But that task is more mundane and time-consuming than running a Pulse Polio campaign. Many more in India survive diarrhoeal attacks but suffer from gastroenteric diseases all through their lives, thus reducing the level of their health. Food security does not consist merely of making foodgrains available to every citizen. The food has to be absorbed in the body to provide nutrition; for this to happen, the body has to be healthy and free of debilitating diseases.

Gloom or Bloom?

As active participants in the major national exercise of 1994–95 conducted by the Technology, Information, Forecasting and Assessment Council (TIFAC) called Technology Vision for India 2020 (TVI 2020), we were very happy to learn from the 5000-odd experts and generalists from various walks of life that India was all set to capture the strength of its endowments in natural resources and human resources, and emerge as a major economic and strategic power in the world. At that time the world was in the throes of a financial crisis, considered to be a major crisis then; it mostly affected the South-East Asian countries which were fast emerging as major economic powers. India was not affected much because it had not globalized until recently, having liberalized its economy only in 1991, after its own serious domestic economic crisis. India's global connections were limited.

But due to the four-decades-long governmental bureaucracy, the Indian citizen had never enjoyed a high economic growth rate. In fact, the growth rate was only slightly more than the rate of growth of the population. Therefore the standard of living for a middle-class or a poor person was quite low. During the discussions for TVI 2020, there were heated debates whenever we had to assume a certain rate of growth for the economy and the Gross Domestic Product (GDP): a 5 per cent growth was considered too ambitious by most economic pundits. We had to arrive at a compromise formula: we tried not to assume technologies which would require a higher growth rate—of 6–7 per cent. It was against such general pessimism—or cautious optimism—that the national exercise was conducted. But as we had projected in our 1998 book *India 2020: A Vision for the New Millennium*, the overall expectations for India turned out eventually to be much higher, probably because for decades after Independence the country's potential had not been tapped fully. Most of those who participated in the TVI 2020 exercise had grown up during the era of planned economy and did not fully understand the forces of liberalization that were freeing the economy up to market forces, and the globalization that was allowing the market forces from other countries to act on our economy as well.

In any case, the basic elements of economic growth also included growth in the technological strengths of all sections of the economy—agriculture, mining, manufacturing, infrastructure and services. The strategic sector too played a crucial role in economic growth.

Instead of going through each element of the economy with a toothcomb, what we did with the Vision 2020 exercise was to give Indians a new way of thinking. After participating in TVI 2020 or reading our book that grew out of it, most Indians started believing that India could become a developed country by the year 2020. Some even started using words like 'Superpower' when talking about India.

India in the World

On the whole, there has definitely been a sea-change in India since 1996, when the TVI 2020 reports were dedicated to the nation by the then prime minister.

India is now the largest producer of milk in the world (it produces about 105 million tonnes per annum). It is the second largest producer of fruits and vegetables (150 million tonnes per annum), the third largest producer of foodgrains (230 million tonnes per annum), and the third largest producer of fish (7 million tonnes per annum). At the time of the Vision 2020 exercise, India was in the second place in milk production.[1] The above achievements (data of 2012–13) are of course laudable, under normal circumstances. However, when one compares these with the figures projected in terms of the consumption needs of our people (with an assumption of the growth of India's population to 1.3 billion by 2020), they fall short by about 30 per cent for milk and about 15 per cent for foodgrains. (In fruits and vegetables they are a close match.) The population may even exceed 1.3 billion by 2020. The trouble with such significant shortfalls is that the per capita consumption of the Indian population remains low.

When we were looking ahead when writing *India 2020*, the production of elements like foodgrains, milk, and the like, was projected to be more, so that India could become an exporter as well. Some exports are taking place now, which is commendable. But these are not yet in adequate quantities to be of help to our own people in terms of providing better earnings. Perhaps the production figures have not caught up with the ones projected in *India 2020* for domestic household consumption. This indicates the sluggishness of income growth. Our reference figures given in *India 2020* (Chapter 4, page 63, Table 4.2) were based on projected household demands assuming a 7 per cent growth in income. The actual growth in incomes has been much lower.

This sluggish growth in incomes must not be attributed to failures in agriculture. Even during the current periods of economic slowdown, the agriculture sector has grown steadily. While one always expects a higher crop yield because of the potential of Indian soils, water resources and our climate, it is mainly in the agricultural sector that growth has been good during the past years. It has been very good for cotton, maize and soya bean.

In fact, when one looks at the rates of growth of agricultural production since 1995, we find that agricultural production has kept up an increase in growth rates throughout. That is good news. Agriculture has done well, but it can do much more. India's poverty can be eliminated only when Indian farmers and farm workers can earn good incomes and become prosperous.

In other sectors, especially in manufacturing, India's performance has been of concern. Even the growth figures projected earlier, before the economic slowdown, were to a large extent dependent on the import of many equipments and materials. The performance of the mining and infrastructure sectors has also been hamstrung for a variety of reasons.

In the mining sector, be it for coal, iron ore, and so on, of which India has plenty, its utilization and scope for value addition have got into knotty problems ranging from environmental clearances and activist protests to administrative delays, court orders and allegations of corruption. One of the key natural resources which gives India its potential strength is remaining idle, without wealth and employment creation. Similarly, many projects in the infrastructure sector have also suffered.

Let us now look at some performance indicators, looked at in the global context.

It will be good to dwell on this table for a while. Let's look first at steel production. The global production in 1997 was 750 million metric tonnes (MMT). China was at 100 MMT, India at 24 MMT. The 2010 projection given in *India 2020* (Chapter 5, page 113, Figure 5.1) was 60 MMT for India— with a query, why not 120 MMT? The lower earlier

TABLE 1.1

Sl No.	Items*	World	China	USA	EU	India	Brazil	South Africa
1.	Steel	1607.20	779.0	87.0	165.60	81.20	34.20	7.22
2.	Chemicals**	3842.00	1029.0	572.2	755.00	108.00	123.00	–
3.	Aluminum	49.70	24.34	4.90	13.20	3.8	1.44	1.00
4.	Milk	724.0	40.0	91.0	210.0	120.0	32.3	3.3
5.	Rice	719.74	204.20	9.00	–	153.00	11.50	26.8
6.	Wheat	671.00	121.00	62.00	196.00	95.00	–	1.9
7.	Major Fruits	287.40	50.30	77.5	39.0	35.0	26.4	3.12
8.	Vegetables	797.0	296.0	66.80	149.4	90.50	10.50	3.44

*In million metric tonnes (MMT)

** In billion US$

Source: CMIE, FAO, Planning Commission, etc., data for 2010. Courtesy Nirmala Kaushik and Sumitra Biswas of TIFAC.

projection was because all of us had to be guided by the commanding heights of public sector steel production, with the Tatas playing a smaller role. Later, the private sector had been given more opportunities. Our 120 MMT target was based on the fact that some experts felt it was easily achievable, due to the abundance of high-quality iron ore. But the actual achievement in 2010 is 81 MMT—not a bad figure, but just compare it with China, which now produces 779 MMT, up from 100 MMT in 1997. Needless to add, steel is the dominant structural material in every sector.

With aluminium we have done better than what we projected in *India 2020* (Chapter 5, page 114, Figure 5.2)—as compared to the projected figure of 1.3 MMT for 2010 (1997 production was 0.6 MMT), we have achieved a production of 3.8 MMT. In chemicals too we have done well, but there is a greater dependence on imported raw materials. Still, our global presence in terms of chemical exports is good.

Table 1.1 should really give us a wake-up call, and we need to heed that call now. The USA and the European Union (EU), with a population of about 350 million each, have figures far better than India in most categories. In most manufactured material items, they have very low per capita energy consumption per tonne and low levels of pollution. This is not the case with China—but see its achievement, with a very large population (like us) of above 1 billion. Are we using our human resources and our endowed natural resources optimally? The answer to that question will determine whether India will be a developed nation and, more importantly, whether India's people will be able to earn better incomes. It is by increased value addition to natural resources that wealth becomes greater. It is the greater wealth which comes through the productive work of people that allows them to have a good life, higher self-respect and better hope for the future.

Let us look another critical factor in the modern economy which is crucial for all sectors including health delivery and education: electric power.

An online search gives us reasonably reliable data about world electricity production. We have taken the figures below from the CIA World Factbook.

These figures speak for themselves. We often ask, what impedes a faster growth for India? Readers can do the math for themselves—the per capita comparison among these countries is easily arrived at by dividing the figures above by the population of the respective countries. While India with its 1.2 billion–strong

TABLE 1.2 Countries in Terms of Electricity Production (in billion kilowatt hour) (as of 1 January 2012)

1.	China	4977
2.	USA	4099
3.	European Union	3255
4.	Russia	1057
5.	Japan	936
6.	India	835

population produces 835 billion KWH, a relatively small country like Israel (about 6 million people) produces 53 billion KWH.

The moment we do the per capita calculations, India's rank in the world falls very low. Let us remember this: it is not enough to take pride in the fact that India is first or second in the world in milk production. It is important to calculate per capita—to see what share of production falls to every citizen.

Gross Domestic Product

There are GDP figures of different kinds, available from various sources. We prefer to use the nominal

GDP figures rather than the PPP (purchasing power parity) figures. PPP figures may look like a palliative sometimes, making us look better. But in reality, in the cost-of-living figures there are many burden assumptions: for example, that the quality of food or water or goods available in different countries are all the same. Let us stick our neck out and compare ourselves directly in nominal dollar terms.

In *India 2020* (pages 11–12, Tables 1.2, 1.3), the world GDP had been projected to be US$ 46,689 billion, assuming an annual growth rate of 2.5 per cent for 1995–2000, 3 per cent for 2000–2010 and 3.5 per cent for 2010–20. The world GDP has in fact grown faster than projected: it now stands at US$ 72,690 billion. The USA heads the list of the top countries of the world according to GDP, with a GDP of US$17,528 billion; China comes second with US$10,028 billion, and Japan third with US$4846 billion. India is tenth on the list with a GDP of US$1996 billion, preceded by Germany, France, UK, Brazil, Italy and Russia.[1]

In *India 2020* we envisaged Big League Countries (BLCs) to be about thirty-eight in number by 2010 and forty-two by 2020—the countries having a GDP of US$ 100 billion or more are defined as BLCs. The good news is that in the UN list there are already sixty countries in the BLC by that definition. Yes, more countries have become wealthier.

India is at the bottom of the top ten GDP list, as we had projected in *India 2020* (page 14, Figure 1.1). It was at the fifteenth position in 1996 and climbed five notches to reach no. 10 in 2010, where it remains in 2012. Our further projection (in *India 2020*) that India would reach the fourth or fifth position was based on an assumed growth rate of 8 per cent during 2007–11 and 9 per cent during 2012–20. With the current slowdown of the Indian economy and serious internal domestic difficulties on many fronts, can we really reach that fourth or fifth position, let alone a third position after China?

Those who are lower than us in the list are not performing badly. A per capita calculation instantly reveals that many of these countries are actually better off than India. The sheer size of our population keeps us on the job because each Indian in the working age and even beyond sixty years does some productive work and adds to the GDP—otherwise they cannot survive. But are they able to produce in a more value-added way, that is the question. The more the value addition, the more the contribution to the GDP.

That is how China has achieved the second position, by enabling many Chinese people to engage in value-added manufacturing, agriculture and services. Note that China is not only a giant in manufacturing and infrastructure but also does very well in agricultural production, as we have seen before. Japan, with around one-tenth of our population, is high on the list despite serious problems that hamper economic growth, some of it due to its ageing population (about one-third of its total population). You can calculate how much more value addition a single Japanese person does in the economy.

When will India reach the standards of such high value-added productive work for the Indian workforce?

Beyond Technology, Economics

As the history of many countries shows, fast economic growth and technological diffusion in society lead to the rapid growth of the middle class, that is, those with better disposable incomes. Their needs are beyond the old clichéd slogans of 'food, clothes, shelter'.

Liberalization and globalization in India post-1991 led to a rapid growth of the middle class. Many young people started getting much higher incomes that what their parents got at the time of retirement. Many young women entered the workforce, especially in the jobs created by the outsourced IT (information technology) industry. Such a rapid growth of better-paying job opportunities had a cascading effect on the economy: people now had access to two-wheelers, cars, processed food, better clothing and footwear with several options, in fact, to a whole set of consumer goods with multiple options. India was no longer a country with the choices only between two kinds of two-wheelers, two brands of cars, one solitary source of cooking-gas cylinders with long waiting times, and one telephone service provider with connection delays of three to four years.

Earlier, most essential goods were rationed, and options were few. And so 'privileged access' through 'connections' was very important. Those who were in their twenties in 1991 suddenly saw a world of plenty. One of the reasons the book *India 2020* caught the national imagination was because the youth with good incomes and even their elders, who had starting working in the 1960s and '70s (struggling all through with scarcities), found a new hope in India. It seemed just within their reach to become citizens of a 'developed country' with good job opportunities and better incomes.

The parents were ready to sacrifice some luxuries to provide good professional education to their children. That was the reason for large enrolments in schools in the higher secondary levels and, more importantly, in the engineering, medical, business management and commerce streams in universities. Most of the new institutions were funded by the private sector and parents paid for the services through escalated fees.

Along with this, there was a sudden rise in entertainment options—a rapid growth in television channels that now numbered 100-plus, a far cry from the single Doordarshan channel of the olden days. Many of the channels were even in different Indian languages.

Without doubt, with liberalization many poor people were raised to the levels of the (lower) middle classes—with a hope that their next generation would achieve middle-class status.

There were many good things happening very rapidly for a few hundreds of millions of Indians. So do expectations rise! People want more and more, and to lead better and better lives. Many more millions who have not yet been covered by these new measures adequately also start expecting, and in some cases demanding, more.

When the system is unable to deliver, there is anger. It is also a natural human tendency to look for culprits. 'Fixing responsibility' becomes the objective. Few realize that the system is much more complex. In a democracy based on constitutional processes, one person cannot take decisions and execute projects single-handedly, however well she or he knows what to do. In addition, no single solution is available off the shelf to be applied to all problems. Life is complex, the economy is complex, and technological processes build up and become effective in a complex manner. Therefore, solutions for problems facing the country are multifaceted.

In cold statistical terms, the nationwide numbers may be small. But one cannot brush away these problems. We, as a nation, need to find solutions depending upon the micro-situations instead of generalizing. At the same time, it is important to remember that what is perhaps good at a micro-level may not necessarily good or needed for all.

Similarly, for an issue like corruption, the solutions are not simple. No doubt there is plenty of scope to simplify the approval and other administrative procedures to reduce the reach of corruption. But even with the reduction of many of the currently existing procedures and approval-inspection cycles, there are some irreducible items on which the executive has to take a decision. Each such decision whose solution is unique cannot be reduced to a simple formula.

One major area of concern is the continuing growth of Indian-owned black money, both within the borders of India and outside. According to a recent (December 2013) news report, over Rs 4 lakh crore of black money went out of India during 2011. This estimate is based on a rigorous methodology by the international watchdog Global Financial Integrity (GFI) tracking various financial transactions around the world. There are various forms of outflow of black money from India, such as smuggling, illegal direct cash transfers, and so on. Estimates on accumulated black money by Indians in other countries and within India vary widely and wildly. Much of it may not be in banks. It may be invested in shares of global companies, properties and other places. Several lakhs of crores of illegal money is floating all over the world. This has serious distorting effects on the economy, on governance, politics, media and several other cultural and social aspects of Indian life. Indian society has to find innovative and pragmatic methods of utilizing this money to create new enterprises in India and therefore job opportunities for Indians. Our guess is that if this is done well, the GDP growth rate will increase by 3 per cent, a much needed booster shot for the slowing economy.

To Sum Up

After the Vision 2020 exercise, India had started marching ahead. Of course others in the world, especially China, stared galloping in the meantime. India went ahead and then, somewhere in between, at the first sight of a good life and better prosperity, we appear to have relaxed somewhat.

However, the fundamental strengths of the Indian economy, national resources and human capabilities still remain. The youthful population is an additional competitive advantage, if prepared and channelized well.

Many projects on the lines stipulated in the Vision 2020 exercise are yet to be taken up. New enterprises may make their presence felt too, and new educational and skill–imparting institutions can make a major difference.

So, are we ready for the future? On your marks . . . get set . . . and go!

CHAPTER 2 | Learning from Missed Opportunities

India is endowed with some wonderful natural resources, which would be enough to support a sizeable part of the earth's population. India's biodiversity is exceptional; there is plenty of sunshine round the year, and a large percentage of the soil is arable. Only a few countries are so fortunate with natural resources.

The people of India are very resilient and have an innate intelligence. They are quick to learn new things and adapt to change rapidly. The way in which cable television and mobile telephones spread to every corner of India within a few years is simply remarkable. Mumbai's dabbawallahs adapted to an opportunity in a newly urbanized Bombay decades ago. Despite general policy neglect, India's farmers and farm workers keep the country's growing population fed, mostly using traditional wisdom, a tenacity to work and the latest farming technologies.

India's civilizational and cultural heritage shows itself in every part of the country. The artefacts left by our ancestors are wonders in the modern world. These are only some of the things that have earned India a special place in the world.

If you look up books or government documents written some five decades ago, you will find many such descriptions of the greatness of the country and its people. In the decades after Independence, many rosy projections were put forward about how these potentials could be converted into benefits. *India 2020* too elaborated on many of India's potentials and looked at how they could be best used for growth and development, and above all for providing prosperity to the people.

What is the progress that has been made in key sectors over the past few decades? If you ask any Indian, the chances are that he or she will list out a number of missed opportunities, along with some impressive achievements.

The Electronics Story

When we think of missed opportunities, many things come to mind at once. But we will start with the area of electronic components, microelectronics and computers.

Homi Bhabha identified electronics as an important element for the future in the 1960s itself; Vikram Sarabhai followed up on Bhabha's vision, creating a Central government department for electronics in the 1970s. At that time, India had a fledgling radio industry with electronic valves. That industry was equal to or better than what South Korea had. Those were the days of accelerating growth in electronics; new industries and new products like integrated circuits (ICs) were just emerging.

In the 1960s, the Tata Institute of Fundamental Research (TIFR) built a valve-based computer. It was one of the first set of computers in the world; it was a major enough achievement to be reported in the annual series of books called *Advances in Electronics* which has global coverage.

And what is the status of microchip manufacturing in India today? Microelectronics and ICs are the blood, flesh and bones of computers and the information technology (IT) industry. A recent article describes the current world situation and the attempts made by the Indian government to attract investors in this sector to India, with many concessions. The article reveals the pathetic fact that 'by 2020 the government expects India to import electronic goods worth almost US$300 billion. The import bill could exceed that of oil'.[1]

What happened to the electronics industry in India? Since the 1970s, through a series of policy measures and procedural hassles, we did not allow foreign companies who had just started manufacturing ICs to set up facilities in India. At the same time, no serious attempts were made to produce major computers within India, with or without foreign collaboration. Arguments ranged from self-reliance ('We should wait for our own India-unique designs to come up and then produce') to concentration on domestic consumption ('Why copy others? We should make things for India—why waste our efforts in exports?').

Both of us vividly remember how much the Indian Space Research Organisation (ISRO) had to struggle to get computers in those days. On ISRO's part, support was given to the Electronics Corporation of India (ECIL) to make local computers (the TDC series) mostly by reverse engineering the PDP computer series. Even with the limited ISRO budget, we procured them from ECIL (along with the developmental costs and technical risks), as a backup for India's first satellite launch vehicle project, SLV-3.

We are aware of various other opportunities in setting up a full-scale microelectronics production facility in India which were missed. Setting up the Semiconductor Complex Ltd (SCL), for instance, was done with limited objectives, not in keeping with the world trends.

Now there is an overabundance of microelectronics in the world, with China and Taiwan becoming global hubs. We have missed the opportunity. The only consolation we have is that 'we have the talent and expertise in designing not just the parts of the chip but in making the complete chip . . . for example, global semiconductor design and manufacturing company Texas Instrument designs the complete chip for its mobile handsets out of its Bangalore facility'.[2] But most manufacturing in large quantities is done outside India; how many high-skilled jobs are lost as a result for Indians?

We were aware of the possibilities of entering into manufacturing microelectronics and computers in India with foreign collaboration, but it was not really on the radar of the decision-makers, who were busy firefighting other, more immediate issues. The damage has now been done: computer and chip imports are going to bleed India's foreign exchange reserves soon.

Even now, some solutions are possible. But it will require a courageous leader to take the necessary steps. India cannot afford to miss out on electronics hardware manufacturing in the country, both for domestic consumption and exports, especially since most modern 'smart' systems, from biomedical equipment to entertainment and security systems have electronic hardware and computer chips at their core.

The IT Infatuation

Similar to the major missed opportunity in electronics is the total neglect of the entire manufacturing sector in India since 1995. The impact of this is much more devastating. Many of our current problems such as the slowdown of the economy and large-scale unemployment are the results of indecisive thinking that went on for decades.

Our politicians, planners, economists and other decision-makers were greatly enamoured by the IT boom in the mid-1990s, which was based on the outsourcing of projects by US companies to India, the work involving a large number of skilled workers. India had the advantage of English-speaking people, and a large and youthful workforce who were happy with the higher incomes they got. The fact that India was on the other side of the globe from the US was an added advantage: when employees in the US closed shop for the day, it was morning in India, and time for the India-based technical workers to pick up the work. In addition, a group of Indian technical workers were willing to work night shifts as well, so that their US counterparts could link with them in real time. Effectively, the Indian workers worked round the clock; it was all 'business at the speed of light' in a 'flat world'.

This was of course a very good business opportunity that we seized; the entrepreneurs and businesspersons who grabbed the opportunity in the years after economic liberalization should be commended. It is also to be noted that India's much-maligned self-financing private sector engineering colleges provided the majority of the vast army of skilled young men and women who took up the outsourced IT jobs. Many of them also went to the US as part of their job. The millions of Indian IT professionals who are in the US, Europe, Australia, Singapore and other global arenas today are not just from the Indian Institutes of Technology (IITs) but also from these other colleges.

Good incomes in the hands of young people had a trigger effect: the purchase of white goods, automobiles, etc., and expenditure on travel, entertainment and personal effects saw a sudden upsurge. Jobs were created in India even for those who did not have a college education. To feed such a huge machinery of new companies, many private sector self-financing schools, colleges, coaching classes, and the like, sprang up as well. The blossoming companies were also job creators and income providers, thus adding to the growth of the GDP. Economists and policymakers were of course happy with these growth figures.

This growth was welcome, no doubt, but the growth envisaged in *India 2020* or the Vision 2020 document was not merely a growth in macro numbers. Our vision included details of possible growth in agriculture, mining, manufacturing, infrastructure, strategic industries and services. It was to be a balanced growth, so that the growth story could be sustained. But those who chase macro numbers are often too impatient to look into the components of the sub-elements. So the areas of micro, small and medium enterprises (MSMEs), hardware manufacturing, value addition in mining, and so on, were ignored as technical details. Furthermore, these sectors were pooh-poohed as sunset industries. The pundits claimed that India, being a country of knowledge, had bypassed the 'dirty' phases of agriculture and manufacturing to directly usher in the era of services-led growth.

One of us was a member of the prime minister's task force on IT set up during the late 1990s. The task force came up with a full set of recommendations for software-based industries and another for hardware (manufacturing). It gave equal importance to both. The software part of the recommendations was accepted without reservations, and all government notifications in this regard came through speedily. This led to the rapid growth of IT-enabled services, the BPO sector, and the like, which was good. But the set of reports that had to do with hardware only gathered dust. It was rumoured that the domestic IT majors requested the government to postpone the hardware initiatives, since their principals (outsourcing US and European companies) might not like India-made hardware to be used in the work outsourced by them, and India might lose some of the outsourced business as a result.

Neglect of Manufacturing

MSMEs and even big manufacturing companies were similarly neglected. The growth of the auto sector and the rising pharmaceuticals sector which had successfully entered global markets were enough to satisfy India's pride in manufacturing. The machine tools sector, which is at the heart of manufacturing, languished. No special efforts were made to create a machine tool manufacturing base in India. Hindustan Machine Tools (HMT), the public sector unit which was created after Independence to produce machine tools, did well initially with imported technologies. But it did not keep up with upgradations, let alone research and development (R&D). At some point, it became a channelizing agent for imports, and was satisfied with agency commissions.

Around 1995, India had a good proportion of local production, but now it is mostly import-dependent as Indian machine tool producing industries are lagging behind in technologies and product engineering. In comparison, China not only tops the world in consumption and local production of machine tools but also ranks high in exports. A decade ago, China relied heavily on imports.

The table below[3] shows India's standing in the world.

Imagine a situation where we want to up the current rate of $2 per capita consumption to a more acceptable global norm, say $15 or $20 per capita. What will the import bill be like?

TABLE 2.1 Top Consumers: Value of machine tools installed in millions of US dollars, 2012 (Est.)

S. No.	Country	Consumption	Change*	$/Capita
1.	China	38,510.2	-1%	$29
2.	United States	8,722.5	19%	$28
3.	Japan	7,462.8	1%	$59
4.	Germany	6,400.2	0%	&78
5.	Korea, Rep. of	4,646.0	-11%	$96
6.	India	2,286.1	2%	$2
7.	Italy	2,172.0	-15%	$37
8.	Brazil	1,867.2	-22%	$9
9.	Taiwan	1,844.0	-7%	$80
10.	Mexico	c1,360.9	0%	$12
11.	Turkey	1,344.3	0%	$18
12.	Russia	1,317.0	0%	$9
13.	Canada	c1,255.6	10%	$37
14.	France	1,118.1	-8%	$17
15.	Switzerland	1,034.4	-14%	$136
16.	United Kingdom	816.2	11%	$13
17.	Austria	586.0	2%	$71
18.	Spain	392.0	-1%	$10
19.	Czech Republic	348.5	-4%	$34
20.	Sweden	344.4	0%	$38

S. No.	Country	Consumption	Change*	$/Capita
21.	Netherlands	343.1	7%	$21
22.	Argentina	261.3	24%	$6
23.	Belgium	246.8	-9%	$24
24.	Romania	c243.0	0%	$11
25.	Australia	210.0	-1%	$10
26.	Finland	140.1	1%	$27
27.	Portugal	137.5	26%	$13
28.	Denmark	39.8	0%	$7

Apparent Consumption = Domestic Production + Imports − Exports
*Change from 2011, measured in reporting currency
Consumption per capita based on 2011 population estimates
c=circa; rough estimate from fragmentary reports

Isn't it clear that we need to prioritize creating an ambience for a high-quality machine production business in India? The major part of this business could be run by multinational companies (MNCs) or as joint ventures with MNCs; what is vital is that a good part of the production is local. The industry would create many jobs. In addition, since machine tools are at the core of manufacturing, the industry would stimulate many MSMEs to come up within India. These units should attempt to export as well, to balance the import bill at least partly.

Stagnant Manufacturing

This is perhaps the biggest story of missed opportunities.

Warning voices were raised on the subject of stagnant manufacturing in India since the turn of the century, but the warnings went unheeded, drowned in the chorus of 'services-led growth'. In recent years, the discourse has become skewed towards 'rights-led development'. The thinking for it goes like this: If people lose jobs due to serious problems in the manufacturing sector, the solution lies in disbursal of some money for 100 days under the employment guarantee scheme. But what happens to the remaining 265 days in the year? Also, where will the money come from if agriculture and the manufacturing sector languish? Agriculture is at least in the hands of individual farmers, so it has subsisted and grown slowly. But even though the bulk of manufacturing is in the unorganized sector, it depends on the availability of raw materials, electricity, energy, transport, and so on; manufacturing as an industry cannot survive without the support of infrastructure.

In a recent e-book on non-manufacturing, the editors conclude:

The Indian manufacturing sector has stagnated and this has adversely affected the growth of employment, investment (both domestic and foreign), and exports. This has created a huge gap between Indian imports and exports, leading to a foreign exchange crisis. The growth of Indian national income cannot be sustained without a vibrant and active manufacturing sector. The main cause of the decline in manufacturing is due to governance and policy slack.[4]

In the same book, N.S. Siddharthan elaborates in his article 'What Ails Manufacturing':

The development experience of most countries, including Europe and Japan, shows manufacturing to be the main engines of growth. During the periods of sustained rapid economic growth, the share of agriculture in national income and the share of agricultural employment in total employment decreases. The space vacated by agriculture is mainly occupied by manufacturing. The share of manufacturing in national income increases rapidly and then stabilizes after reaching about 30 per cent. After this the services sector takes over.[5]

This is a very clear articulation of the dynamics between the three major sectors.

In India, the share of agriculture came down to about 14.6 per cent in 2009–10 from 28.9 per cent in 1993–94. Manufacturing went up from 14.2 per cent in 1993–94 to 15.9 per cent in 2009–10. Services went up from 44.1 per cent in 1993–94 to 57.3 per cent in 2009–10.[6]

As N.S. Siddarthan points out, the services sector is a mixed bag: it includes IT services and government salaried services, but much of the rest of the sector is unorganized, comprising the self-employed poor who live on subsistence wages.

In India the agriculture sector has not stopped growing, even if the growth has been slow. But people are not able to move from agriculture to manufacturing, since the latter sector is stagnant. So the Indian poor are forced to earn a living in the slow-moving, low-income agriculture sector which is unable to offload the excessive people dependent on it (the rural poor). Meanwhile, manufacturing, including the unorganized manufacturing sector, is stagnating (affecting the urban and rural poor). In the services sector (which employs the urban poor), the lot of the subsistence-wage service provider or the self-employed poor worker hasn't seen any improvement at all. The services sector itself has not seen stable growth, and its growth has been increasingly stunted in recent times.

Where are we headed? Can government services and IT services alone save the Indian people by giving them decent jobs and incomes? That is hardly likely. What is needed urgently is a policy to help Indian MSMEs acquire technical capabilities.

Agriculture

India still had to import substantial quantities of food five to six years ago; it is today the largest exporter of rice in the world, and the second largest exporter of wheat and sugar; export earnings from agriculture are about Rs 232,000 crore a year.[7] The demands made on the agriculture sector by the Food Security Bill mean that we have no choice but to produce more. This involves investing in irrigation, electricity, research and development and infrastructure.

GM crops can come to our aid in a big way. If we look at the genetically modified Bt cotton, the benefits of GM crops become clear. Seven years ago, India was importing cotton; today, we are the world's second largest exporter of the crop.[8]

If we do not miss opportunities like these in agriculture and plan effectively, rural poverty could soon be a thing of the past.

Time to Give Up or Time to Start Anew?

These instances of missed opportunities should wake us up. The reason India missed these opportunities was not because we were waiting for new discoveries of science or new engineering inventions. Many of the missed opportunities were a result of imaginary fears about incurring losses, an imaginary pride that we would find an India–unique path for everything, a misplaced arrogance of not wanting to learn from others, and a total neglect of the pragmatic needs of the poor.

Are we ready to learn from other countries? Are we ready to move fast now, after we have missed decades of progress? Or are we happy to be a continual underperformer, covering up the real state of affairs with statistical jugglery for public consumption?

In this context it is interesting to look at a particularly clear analysis of data in an article in the *Business Standard* last year.[9] The author compares the boom years of India's economy with the economies of the East Asian tigers (China, Taiwan, Indonesia, Malaysia, Thailand, South Korea, Singapore).

> Over the longer (post-1979) period, Indian growth was utterly unremarkable compared to Asian peers. But even the India Shining years seem less glossy. In real time, the impression was one of India outperforming all countries except China. Properly measured, India did well but not as well as the Asian tigers during their comparable growth spurts.

Somewhere in the article he points out that had India not underperformed, India's per capita GDP would have been $15,000 instead of $4000. That is the sum of our losses from missed opportunities.

At this point we would like to quote a passage from something we wrote sixteen years ago in *India 2020* (p.154):

> During the five decades after independence we had so many major problems to solve. Looking back we have also not had the type of resolve that is required to wipe out the centuries of stagnation and emerge as a vibrant society. We have let go many opportunities presented by technologies, as well as by trade and business. Missed opportunities do not usually recur

in the same form. In a competitive world, there are others waiting to seize these opportunities. Much more than the blows to national pride or that of the intellectuals, the worst outcome of such missed opportunities is the loss to the nation. Slow economic growth hits the poor the most. Our utmost attention during the next quarter century should be to attend to these problems of growth and removal of poverty. In order to do so, we may have to adapt many things from the world, as also prepare ourselves for future creative adventures.

Other countries keep growing too, though their growth rate may slow down when they reach higher levels. But we are still at a lower level. We need to sprint a marathon for two decades in order to catch up.

Are you ready? We think that young Indians are ready, ready not to miss any opportunity, and instead grab every chance with both hands.

The time for change is now. The alternative is clear, and dire. If we continue in the present mode, others in the world will overtake us. We will be caught in balance-of-payment problems. And, above all, poverty and unemployment will increase further, leading to an implosion of our society.

And if we make the change, we can make real progress: from subsistence levels to sustained satisfactory levels; from poverty to prosperity; from stagnation to speedy growth.

It is time to start anew, to get set and go.

In the next chapter we will see how we can build up the momentum.

3 Accelerating Agricultural Growth

For most Indians in urban areas and even in intellectual debates in the media, food availability is something that is taken for granted. Many of us seem to have forgotten that our country saw widespread famines around the time of Independence, and even in the 1960s there were severe food shortages and rationing. It is the success of the agriculture sector that has enabled our sense of food security.

It was the Green Revolution in the late 1960s, initiated boldly by the late C. Subramaniam, that changed the picture with regard to food availability. There were no longer any nationwide crises requiring a 'ship-to-mouth' existence. We were no longer dependent on food shipments from the US to avert serious food shortages.

By the time we wrote *India 2020* in 1998, food availability was no longer an issue. But those who produced the food, namely the farmers and farm workers, who along with their families formed about two-thirds of India's population, were not in a very good situation. Large- and medium-size farmers were well off, but most others—who were a large majority, about 70 per cent of the overall number of farmers— were marginal farmers, owning small plots of lands.

Also, the spread of the Green Revolution had halted by the 1990s, confining the major granaries to Punjab, Haryana, western Uttar Pradesh and Andhra Pradesh, where the high-yield agriculture was beginning to show problems of fatigued soil. The input costs needed to get good yields were going up.

The Vision 2020 team led by the late Prof. S.K. Sinha looked at these issues holistically. Their key recommendations are worth repeating here (reproduced from *India 2020*, Chapter 4, pages 84–85).

- India to aim to be a major player in the world in the agricultural sector and a leading exporter of grains and other agri-products.
- Eastern India to become a major producer of wheat.
- Rice-producing areas to use hybrid seeds on a large scale.
- Central India to be made a centre of vegetables, fruits, pulses and coarse grains.

- More emphasis on tuberous crops.
- Water as a national resource—water management as the key to agricultural prosperity.
- Core post-harvest technologies to be mastered and disseminated.
- Steps to educate farmers about what is happening elsewhere, if need be by providing them the opportunity to travel, and use of space technologies to facilitate interaction and encourage farmers to ask questions and share experience.

How does one express the vision for agricultural prosperity, describe a vision which uses all the advantages of agro-climate and natural resources, with the use of right and continuous doses of modern technology? The vision naturally includes the fact that for all Indians the availability of food and worrying about where the next meal is coming from will no longer be a prime concern. They will have food in plenty compared to their situation today.

A vision for total production or per capita consumption or export figures alone does not comprise the totality of what we envisage. The action taken to realize it is just as important. Achieving these projections is not at all impossible. Investments are not difficult. But there is a lot of hard work, synchronization of policies, administrative support and actual field work which includes taking people and farmers into confidence and reaching the benefits of technologies to them that is required.

What Is the Progress?

The good news is that the direction of actions taken by the Central government, the state governments and several other stakeholders are almost on the lines summarized above. But progress has to be accelerated. We should be quick to point out though that in spite of the several constraints that have been placed on the agri-sector, it is the one sector that has kept the Indian economy from collapsing. For the past two years, when the industrial sector came close to zero growth, it was the agri-growth that kept the overall GDP growth at a respectable level.

We will quickly review some elements of the progress and problems in the following paragraphs, before concluding what can be done in this sector and how soon.

The target of agricultural growth for the eleventh Five Year Plan (2007–12) was 4 per cent. The achieved rate is 3.5 per cent. As per the Vision 2020 estimates, even the targets fixed for the eleventh Plan were small: we need to fix more aggressive targets as they are achievable. But recall again the last paragraph of the quote from *India 2020* reproduced above. To achieve these targets we need systematic and synchronized actions. We will come to that a little later.

The achievements in agriculture can be seen in India's Economic Survey 2012–13:

- Foodgrain production in India has shown remarkable improvement in recent years. The year 2011–12 saw a record high of 259.32 million tonnes.
- The availability of certified quality seeds more than doubled in 2012–13 from 2005–06.
- The livestock sector achieved an average growth rate of 4.8 per cent.
- Export of agriculture and allied products during 2011–12 accounted for 9.08 per cent of India's total exports against 6.9 per cent during 2010–11.

One of the important achievements during the eleventh Plan period is making eastern India a major supplier of cereal to the Indian market. The other notable fact is that vegetables and fruits are now becoming part of the daily diet of more and more Indians.

On the irrigation front, the situation remains unchanged. The rate of growth of irrigated lands is very slow. About 60 per cent of all agricultural land in India is still rain-fed, that is, dependent on the monsoon. According to the India Brand Equity Foundation (IBEF) reports, 'the increase in the area under irrigation is considerably smaller in comparison to the increase in private and public sector investments.'[1] Thus, an increase in agricultural production achieved now (as described above), can be vulnerable to failures of the monsoon and/or continued drought periods. That is why one of the key recommendations we made in *India 2020*, reproduced earlier in this chapter, was regarding the availability of water to the farmer: water management.

As an important part of the Green Revolution, farmers in irrigated lands used the available water innovatively, bringing India's agricultural production to a fairly good shape, as we had noted in *India 2020*. But that is not the full potential of Indian agriculture. The other agricultural lands, which are almost twice the size of the irrigated areas, need to be enabled with water availability through micro- and minor irrigation systems and more importantly through drip and sprinkler irrigation methods. Some progress has been made in this area, even if it has been a slow start. The millions of poor, marginal and small farmers who work in the rain-fed agricultural areas have to be provided the minimum water and unique seeds for their particular agricultural conditions.

Again, the use of chemical fertilizers in India compared to the global standards of most developed and emerging countries is reasonable but rather low. The use of pesticides (kilograms per hectare of arable land) is similarly on the lower side. Detailed worldwide comparisons can be had from the data of the World Bank, the Food and Agricultural Organization (FAO) and many other sources that are available on the Internet: interested readers could look at some of these. What we would like to point out is that the consumption of fertilizers, pesticides, and so on, will come to the correct levels in India if agriculture grows and proper water availability is achieved.

Despite more than six decades of discussions and the special emphasis laid in the Vision 2020 documents on water management (which can be self-sustaining, as was demonstrated by Prof. S.K. Sinha and his team in several parts of India), the 'rain-fed' agricultural lands of India are yet to be taken care of. This is why the rate of growth of agriculture is slow; with monsoon forecasts for 2014 not being favourable, the growth rate might go down further. It is easily possible to reach a steady sustainable growth rate of 5 per cent for Indian agriculture. We will discuss how towards the end of this chapter.

Right now we will turn our attention to another big-ticket item for uplifting Indian agriculture—the use of GM seeds and genetic engineering methods for Indian agriculture.

GM Crops: A Boon for the Farmer

There are many books, articles and news reports about GM crops, debating the pros and cons. It becomes a highly sensitive and explosive issue at times.

Nowadays, in India, anything relating to genetic engineering or genetic modification or transgenic crops tends to become controversial. People seem to have preconceived notions on the subject, and informed debates do not occur.

At the time when the Technology Vision 2020 task forces were doing their research and surveys, GM crops were being experimented with. The task forces had assessed the benefits of GM crops for India. It will be interesting to recall what they had to say as far back as the mid-1990s.

This is what we wrote about the use of biotechnology in *India 2020* (Chapter 4, pages 67–69), based on the findings of the task forces:

We would naturally start with biotechnology as it deals with many aspects of basic inputs to agriculture: seeds, plants, soil treatment, etc. It is crucial to food security, if we take the right steps. One of the most important technologies is that which can lead to transgenic plants; that is, plants which are 'human-made' and are tailored to meet the desired objectives by transfer and expression of the desired type of gene to a target plant. Worldwide, a number of such developments are taking place. In 1994–95, of the total number of 482 transgenic plants that were produced, 30 per cent were field tested for herbicide resistance, 24 per cent for product quality, 21 per cent for insect resistance, 14 per cent for viral resistance, 3 per cent for fungal resistance and 8 per cent for other special traits. Crops reported to have been transformed are vegetables, field crops, fruits and nuts besides others. Among the vegetables are: asparagus, carrot, cauliflower, cabbage, celery, cucumber, horseradish, lettuce, pea, potato and tomato. Among field crops: alfalfa, corn, cotton, flax, oilseed (rape), rice, rye, soyabean, sugarbeet and sunflower. And among fruits/nuts were apple, pear and walnut. . . .

In India, a certain amount of crop (transgenic) biotechnology is being put to use. Major efforts are being undertaken to make cotton pest-resistant. Most readers would be aware of the spate of suicides by cotton farmers recently. Let us hope there will be scientific and technological breakthroughs in pest-resistant transgenic cotton seeds. Till we achieve success in this on a commercial scale we cannot be sure that we will have enough supplies to plan large-scale operations. No doubt such researches should be encouraged, but we should look at other fronts too. It is necessary for research on crop biotechnology in India to be focussed on our important crops, especially those related to food security.

We have to bear in mind that the application of biotechnology may not have any major impact on food security in India in the next five years, though crops of industrial value and vegetables may benefit to some extent.

Since then, a number of rapid developments have taken place worldwide and in India as well. In an excellent article,[2] Clive James has surveyed the whole set of GM crops, covering the period 1996–2000.

He starts with the unprecedented rapid adoption of transgenic crops during the five-year period when GM crops were first adopted, which reflects the significant multiple benefits realized by large and small farmers in industrial and developing countries that have grown transgenic crops commercially. Between 1996 and 2000, a total of fifteen countries—ten industrial and five developing—contributed to more than a twenty-five-fold increase in the global area of transgenic crops, from 1.7 million hectares (ha) in 1996 to 44.2 million ha in 2000. James goes on to say that 'adoption rates for transgenic crops are unprecedented and are the highest for any new technologies for agricultural industry standards'. This is because of a variety of benefits to the users, including improved seed and pest control, reduced expenditure on such controls and ease of operations.

An article in *Nature* magazine provides the current data on the area used for GM crops.[3] Of the total arable land worldwide which is about 1.5 billion ha, 170 million ha is used to cultivate GM crops in twenty-eight countries, as of 2012. Most crops are grown in just five countries: USA, Brazil, Argentina, Canada and India. The land used for GM crops in these five countries amounts to 152 million ha. The other twenty-three countries which are on the list are likely to accelerate the use of the GM mode.

The most popular GM crops are soya bean, cotton, maize and canola. For soya bean about 81 per cent of the crops are in GM mode and only 19 per cent is produced in the conventional mode. For cotton, again, GM crops cover 81 per cent of production, with only 19 per cent in the conventional mode. For maize 35 per cent is in GM mode while 65 per cent is in the conventional mode. For canola it is 30 per cent in GM mode, and 70 per cent conventional.

In 2003–04 Bt cotton (which is a GM crop) contributed 1.23 per cent to the total cotton cultivation of 1.37 lakh bales in India. In 2012–13, it was 91 per cent of the total, which had shot up to 3.52 lakh bales. With the adoption of the GM mode, the yield had more than doubled in nine years.

In the coming years, there will be a large-scale adoption of GM crops by many more countries. We hope India does not lose its momentum in this area where we have found high yield and good applications.

Let us look at GM crops from another angle. In *India 2020* we had emphasized the importance of food security: it is critical for poor and marginal farmers. We would now like to share the results of a recent research survey based on a study of Indian cotton farmer households in four rounds between 2002 and 2008, in Maharashtra, Karnataka, Andhra Pradesh and Tamil Nadu. These four states, according to the researchers, cover a wide variety of different cotton-growing situations—both GM and conventional. They produce 60 per cent of all the cotton in central and south India. It is exciting to see the findings of the survey:

> The results of the research confirm that the income gains through Bt Cotton adoption amongst small holder farm households in India have positive impacts on food security and dietary quality. GM crops are not a panacea for the problems of hunger and malnutrition. Complex problems require multi-pronged solutions. But the evidence suggests that GM crops can be an important component in a broader food security strategy. So far, food security impacts are still confined to only a few concrete examples. The national benefits could further increase with more GM crops and traits becoming available in the future. Appropriate policy and regulatory frameworks are required to ensure that the needs of poor farmers

and consumers are taken into account and that undesirable social consequences are avoided.[4]

So, GM crops are good news not only for the overall economy of the country, such as enhanced production and exports, but also at the micro level, benefiting small households, where increased incomes lead to better food and nutritional security. The country therefore has to take up GM crops in a big way. Our farmers have shown the way through Bt cotton. They can also work wonders with other crops once these are fully tested and released through the national technical agencies. As David Zilberman writes in a recent article:

> GM varieties provide new means to increase crop productivity and are essential in the transition to a renewable, bio-based economy. India's strong scientific base is likely to make it a leader in this new economy. I hope that India will take advantage of the opportunities provided by bio-technology and develop a system that enables the introduction and adoption of GM varieties.[5]

We must not lose this window of opportunity for our farmers and for India.

Structural Changes to Governance in Agriculture

Now we come to a critical item for liberating Indian agriculture and allowing it to reach its full potential: economic reforms in agriculture.

Many of us may not be fully aware of the extent of government control on agriculture. When a farmer produces more, there is no guarantee that he will be able to sell his produce at the best price. There are government orders regarding payments to farmers, and controls on the movement of produce outside a state or even a district. On the other hand, when a farmer loses a season's crop due to poor or untimely rains, there is no easy way of compensating him. There are insurance schemes but the procedure is so complex that the farmer might get his due only after a year.

In our desire to romanticize agriculture and the farmer, we tend to sometimes forget the fact that the overall population of India has increased since Independence by about five times. Though at the time of Independence the workforce depending on agriculture was about 80 per cent, with the five-fold increase it is still at about 60 per cent. That is the reason for large-scale fragmentation of land and the resultant increase in the numbers of marginal farmers. Due to this marginalization of arable lands, youth in many parts of India leave the villages to take up even a low-end service sector job in towns and cities.

Agriculture in India is also suffering from a lack of investment. The government cannot invest effectively in this sector; if it does, it will carry with it lots of bureaucracy, red tape and resultant corruption. And the existing laws are too complex, and there is too much uncertainty involved, for an investor to take up large stretches of marginal lands on a contract basis for agriculture.

A possible solution may lie in large farmers' cooperatives, like the 400-acre, Rs 4000–crore township of Magarpatta near Pune built by farmers on their erstwhile land. The farmers are shareholders in the cooperative that owns the arable land as well as the township built on part of that land. They earn profits both from the agricultural produce and the commercial assets in the township.

The model for such ventures has already been tested out through successful cooperatives in other sectors. Cooperatives like Amul have helped the animal husbandry sector by creating collection centres at the village level and by using high-technology infrastructure for treating milk, packaging and delivery. Such cooperatives in various states produce processed products too, thus increasing the value addition. For sugar-cane production too there are successful examples of such cooperatives in some states, where sugar mill owners work closely with farmer cooperatives to enable both the supply chain and sugar-cane delivery to the mills. The farmers benefit from this arrangement, and so does the industrialist.

This idea for restructuring agriculture may be simple, but it is a powerful idea. It would be wonderful if we were to try it out.

A New Era of Agricultural Prosperity

It is time India marches ahead on agricultural growth, picking up momentum from its current speed. We are happy to note that some states—it is important to remember that agriculture is a state subject—have sped away from the conventional growth rate of about 3 per cent. In a recent article, Ashok Gulati, who is a professor of agriculture in the Indian Council of Research on International Economic Relations, underlines the increased growth rates of agriculture in Gujarat (9.8 per cent), Rajasthan (9.6 per cent),

Chhattisgarh (8.9 per cent), Madhya Pradesh (7.4 per cent) and Jharkhand (6.9 per cent).[6] He says they have all 'registered an impressive growth of almost 7 per cent or higher over a decade-long period. It is not necessary that all states of India need to reach such rates. But they can all improve substantively depending upon their natural endowments . . . If one could learn only a few lessons from this and get all-India GDP growth up to 5 per cent which is achievable provided one takes some bold policy decisions—India will be a different country.'

We need not expand on this statement—it articulates perfectly what we strongly believe. Can we urge our decision-makers to act and our analysts to stop arguing for a while, and give India a chance for a decade?

To sum up, our action plan to accelerate growth in agriculture would include these critical elements:

• Make all rain-fed arable lands of India irrigated in some form: through micro-irrigation, drip or sprinklers, and so on. These have to be provided by the government just as it invested in big dams and irrigation canals earlier. A 90 per cent coverage of all arable lands within a decade should be the target.

- As an allied requirement, 24×7 availability of electric power for all agricultural and irrigation-related activities should become a critical target.

- Following from these, there will be a large flow of technologies and innovations into agriculture. Special steps need to be taken by government agencies through national agricultural institutions, NGOs, private sector companies and others to help the farmers and farm workers with necessary new skills. If we forget this human-resource reskilling, the gains may be lower. Whenever we attempt to increase productivity and efficiency, we should remember it can only be done through a skilled workforce, whatever the equipment, technology and materials used in the process.

- Continual improvement of supply chains is vital. Therefore road infrastructure and communication infrastructure to farm areas are key. They need to be continuously upgraded. Special storages may be required for some agri-products.

- More GM varieties should be given an opportunity to be introduced to Indian farmers. There has to be a continual awareness creation. Indian institutions and industries should be encouraged to generate commercial-level GM varieties out of Indian innovations; this can give us a competitive advantage. Initially, for some more years, we will have to depend upon the GM varieties developed by foreign companies with local production capabilities.

- Continual R&D may be done for cleaner and 'greener' agriculture including organic farming, which may emerge some decades later.

- For all the above, under agriculture we also include animal husbandry, poultry farming and fisheries, efforts on all of which need to be stepped up. But all these are supplementary to the core of land-based, plant-based agriculture.

- Special attention needs to be given to the growing of pulses. India (in fact all of South Asia) has a special love for pulses, as we pointed out in *India 2020*, and it still imports a lot of pulses.

- As agriculture becomes more and more technology-intensive, from seeds to agri-implements to chemicals to software which may be used for various monitoring and control systems, it is necessary to protect India's intellectual properties (IP). IP rights may become crucial to gain a competitive edge in the future. Many products that we use in India today are based on IPs of other countries; we should start generating commercially stable IPs in the country.

- As India becomes competitive at the world level (for domestic consumption or for export markets) there will be competitive pressures built up on the country's products. (Look at the regulating pressures on our pharma products as they started becoming successful in exports and in Indian markets.) There are many provisions in the World Trade Organization (WTO) that may be invoked against India. This is where our government-funded institutions and universities must help the farmers. Our policymakers should also be alert to protect them in global markets, instead of engaging in near-crisis operations as we do now.
- Lastly, we need to take steps towards agricultural cooperatives along the lines discussed earlier. We need to experiment and build institutional frameworks so that Indian agriculture can reach its fullest potentials. We also need our talented youth to become a part of the agricultural revolution, just as they compete for IT jobs now!

Yes, with Indian agriculture growing at a fast rate of 5 per cent or above and reaching its full potential, we will indeed see a different India within a decade. The effects of this will be far-reaching, extending to other sectors and boosting the economy as a whole.

CHAPTER 4 Manufacturing
Mega Possibilities

Manufacturing is the backbone of any reasonably sized country. It can absorb a whole spectrum of skilled workers, from semi-skilled workers to highly accomplished professionals. For a country that aspires to shed its 'underdeveloped' tag, there is a need to siphon off excessive personnel dependent on subsistence agriculture, working as marginal farmers or landless agricultural labourers. Manufacturing is a very good industry to absorb them, making them economically more productive and therefore allowing them to earn more than what they did before.

If one looks back, the earliest industries in India grew around rice milling, jute, sugar, leather and textiles. Even now textile manufacturing is the second

63

largest source of employment after agriculture in India and contributes up to 14 per cent of the industrial production.[1]

When discussing the manufacturing sector, it is the big industries that come to mind; automobile manufacturing is the first thing that comes to mind since its growth has been remarkable in the post-liberalization era. But we should bear in mind that it is the MSMEs that form the backbone of India's employment generation. The MSMEs' contribution to the economy is about 8 per cent of GDP; their share is close to 45 per cent of the total manufactured output in the country and 40 per cent of manufactured exports. About 60 million persons are gainfully employed in the MSMEs which comprise about 26 million enterprises. All is not well with the 26 million enterprises, however, nor is life easy for their 60 million employees. If manufacturing in India is to become healthy, strong and vibrant, urgent attention would need to be given to this sector.

That does not mean that the other large part of the manufacturing sector, namely the big industries, can be forgotten. They are equally important to make this sector a powerful engine for Indian prosperity.

A Quick Recap of the *India 2020* Projections

Our book *India 2020* provided a vision for the manufacturing sector in Chapter 7. It forecast machine tool production for 2010 to be 60 per cent of the manufacturing sector, increasing by 2020 to 80 per cent. This estimate was based on the fact that India had started consuming machine tools in a major way. However, as we have discussed in Chapter 2, India's per capita consumption of machine tools is very low at just $2 (see Table 2.1). That is the index of our manufacturing strengths including that of MSMEs. A big mission lies ahead of us.

Another item envisaged in the Vision 2020 exercises was the vastly increased local production of machine tools in India, even if it was under foreign licence. That too has not materialized. Around 1995, local production accounted for about 80 per cent of local consumption. Now the pie of local consumption has become much larger, but 80 per cent of the tools are imported. Naturally, the other part of the Vision 2020 projections, which was about introducing some of our own India-made software as small incremental innovations to these computer-controlled machines, has not been realized even on a small scale.

Primarily, Indian manufacturing post-liberalization has grown through the import of equipment and technologies, just as it had done earlier. The only difference is that earlier such imports went through the inefficient, time-consuming bureaucratic processes of approval by the offices of the Directorate General of Technology Development (DGTD), whereas now the decision-making power rests with the industries themselves.

In addition, a number of foreign companies have set up facilities in India for downstream engineering products. Still, for major capital goods, there is not much of a presence of foreign companies or MNCs.

Thus, for all engineering sectors including textiles, most of the equipment and machinery is still imported. The Delhi Metro which is a great engineering feat, accomplished thanks to the superb project management capabilities of E. Sreedharan, imported all its equipment, coaches, and so on. Nothing was manufactured locally. This is not the fault of Indian industries. The country has not given enough attention to the growing technological strengths of Indian enterprises, be it in the public or the private sector. That is the reason why even major defence industries continue to import their specialized transport systems.

Thus on the whole our forecast in *India 2020* that 'India will become a net exporter of technologies by 2010' has not materialized. We had made two specific projections, that software development for process and systems will take place, and that 'India will be self-sufficient in advanced machine tools and boilers using state-of-the-art technologies. Exports of these items will progressively increase' (Chapter 7, pages 146–47). Neither of these has come true.

Part of our predictions, that production in India would increase as foreign companies and MNCs set up facilities here, has however become a reality. For example, Hyundai, the Korean automobile manufacturer, not only meets domestic demands in India from its Indian operations now but also exports engines made in India.

But the net result of the stunted growth in this sector is that India's manufactured exports have a low-technology intensity; a recent survey by the ministry of commerce confirms this.

Indian Companies Abroad

Still, it is not the end of the road for the manufacturing sector in India. As per an IBEF document, India ranks fourth in the world in the Global Manufacturing Competitiveness Index (GMCI) in 2013.[2]

Another interesting data from the IBEF report is that India is second only to Japan in the number of companies awarded for quality excellence globally. This is a rigorous process and as tough as it gets for assessing the quality of products. One of the apex awards is the Deming Excellence Award; no less than twenty-one Indian companies have won it. Another 153 Indian companies have won the Total Productive

TABLE 4.1 Global Manufacturing Competitive Index (GMCI) for 2013

Current Rank	Country	Index Score
1.	China	10.00
2.	Germany	7.98
3.	USA	7.84
4.	India	7.65
5.	South Korea	7.59
6.	Taiwan	7.57
7.	Canada	7.24
8.	Brazil	7.13
9.	Singapore	6.64
10.	Japan	6.60

Source: Deloitte and US Council on Competitiveness, Aranca Research

Maintenance (TPM) excellence award. This speaks very highly of the management of these companies and their employees (we must not forget that many of the workers are in fact contract employees). It reinforces our belief that Indian workers, supervisers and managers are indeed world-class.

Indian companies investing abroad is not a new phenomenon. But the present volume and scope of investments are unprecedented. The Birla Group was the first Indian company which went out to Ethiopia back in 1959 to establish a textile mill. Others followed later in other countries. As per the IBEF report quoted above, a majority of the outbound ventures during the 1970s, 1980s and 1990s were medium-sized. The overall investment between 1975 and 1990–91 was about US$220 million. Indian overseas investments have risen since the late 1990s. Between the five financial years (FY) 2006 and 2010 the aggregate outflow of Indian foreign direct investment (IFDI) was about US$72 billion. After a little slowdown IFDI picked up again and touched US$16.8 billion in FY 2011 alone. Now India ranks twenty-first in the world in terms of the magnitude of FDI outflows. On the basis of the value of net purchases—cross-border acquisition deals undertaken by domestic companies in

2010—India figured among the top five globally after USA, Canada, Japan and China. Indian public sector units are also making greenfield investments abroad.[3]

FDI outflows from Indian companies have supported the economies of the host nations in many ways: inducing capital formation, transfer of technical and managerial knowledge and employment generation. As per the estimates of Europe India Chamber of Commerce (EICCI), investments worth €43 billion made by Indian enterprises between 2003 and 2012 led to a creation of 40,000 new jobs in greenfield projects in Europe. Indian management has had a decent track record and proven experience of turning around sick units acquired in foreign countries.

The Indian performance abroad should make us all proud. We believe in global interactions, transactions, sharing and exchanges. India has suffered too long because of its inward-looking, over-centralized, control-era mindset. The energies of our entrepreneurs and investors have suffered seriously as a result. Our youth have faced problems because of running from pillar to post to get a job placement; even skilled workers have not had job security.

The lack of planning and infrastructure are to blame in a large part for this. In addition, Indian labour laws, conceived in the late nineteenth and early twentieth centuries, have simply not kept pace with the drastic changes that have taken place around the world in technologies and business practices. A World Bank report states:

> Indian labour regulations—among the most restrictive and complex in the world—have constrained growth of the formal manufacturing sector where these laws have their mildest application. Better designed labour regulations can attract more labour-intensive investment and create jobs for India's unemployed millions and those trapped in poor quality jobs. Given the country's momentum of growth, the window of opportunity must not be lost in improving the job prospects for the 50 million new entrants who are expected to join the work force over the next decade.[4]

To cap all the above difficulties, a number of new tax laws have complicated the already difficult business climate. The result is that, as numerous studies have established, India is almost at the bottom of the pile among major countries of the world when we look at the ease of doing business.

In this context, the large-scale Indian investments abroad should not be merely seen as a regular venture of an enterprising business person or organization. Behind the impetus for investing abroad is the stark reality that Indian governance systems and infrastructural hurdles are exasperating our enterprises within the country. That is the reason why even in the domestic manufacturing sector there is a slowdown. Several Indian MSMEs are packing up and many of them are now becoming agents for purchasing cheaper goods from China and other manufacturing hubs and selling these in India. This is a dangerous trend because if this goes on, there will be severe job losses in the existing workforce as well as near-zero creation of new jobs.

A Wake-Up Call

Yes, there are alarms ringing all over India—an urgency to wake up and take action now. The intent of action would not be to stop our businesses from investing abroad, but to make India a great destination for investors in manufacturing—not just in the automobile sector, but in machine tools in the MSMEs as well. It is important to remember that while technologies are an important prerequisite for manufacturing growth, the current crises are more due to lack of governance, complicated tax laws, unfair labour laws, lax project management of approved projects, and so on.

Here is our action plan for manufacturing, with the points that the Central and state governments need to focus on immediately:

- Rationalize the tax regimes to make manufacturing and value addition in India an attractive proposition rather than carrying on importing and trading. A lot can be done even within the existing WTO regimes.
- Examine why the approved projects are not taking off or going too slowly. Remove the bottlenecks so that they can be sped up. This is to be done for both private and public sector units.
- The MSMEs need the greatest attention as they contribute a considerable amount to the GDP and more importantly are a great absorber of different types of workers—from low-skilled labourers to high-skilled professionals. We should also create conducive conditions for our educated youth to start knowledge-intensive manufacturing ventures in India, with MSMEs as a base.
- Some parts of the earlier MSMEs have become obsolete and uncompetitive, or even sick. There is

no use in trying to revive such units. But we need to help the investors or some others to create new MSMEs in their place and absorb some of the workforce by reskilling them.

- 'Creative destruction' is a part of modern technological growth and innovative business. It is the responsibility of the government to use modern methods of technology foresight and business forecasts to assess well in advance the changes that are emerging. To help entrepreneurs and the workers to adapt to these changes is the duty of the government. Of course, the industries and scientific and technological institutions also have to reorient themselves and collaborate in the processes.

- The approval cycles for various clearances need drastic changes to enable industries to go ahead with a project within three months of the initial proposal.

- Some of the provisions of the recently enacted Land Acquisition Act need to be kept in abeyance for at least a decade to help manufacturing industries establish themselves.

- So also with many provisions of environmental laws and procedures which need to be industry-friendly.

- But the basic intent of these laws is to protect the people who sell their lands to industries or whose lands are acquired. This needs to be respected and their needs must be taken care of by other means, by giving them productive employment and reasonable incomes.

- Similarly, we need to look differently at tree plantation, protecting water resources, and so on. We need to find new geographies for these, freeing up the space required for manufacturing plants. These could be converted into profitable commercial forests, and many new jobs would be created in the process.

- Our labour laws need considerable revision to ensure maximum employment (with reasonable incomes) as against the current protection of only those workers who are in the organized industry sector. Actions for this are required both at the Central and state government levels.

- There is a need for activists and NGOs to shed their one-point agenda of protests to enable stimulation of the manufacturing sector.

- Our aim should be to have about 100 mega manufacturing Indian companies, many of them listed among the world's top 500 in terms of size and profitability.

- Our traditional strengths in manufacturing like

textiles, leather, gems and jewellery need a renewed focus.

- Agro-goods processing industries and agro-waste harvesting industries need a special fillip.

- An area which is neglected so far in practical terms is the domestic production of defence-related equipment. These need not always be the results of indigenous R&D and designs. We have to build a defence complex in India. Local production of defence equipment will not only create jobs in the short term, but if managed well can also create a highly skilled human capital in India. Indians, as we have pointed out before, are quick to learn and fast to adapt to new methods. If such a highly skilled human capital is developed here, other entrepreneurs can utilize the workforce for their own new enterprises, especially hi-tech industries, which would be a great value addition. This is one way in which the country's manufacturing strengths could grow at great speed.

- In order to achieve the above, various policy and procedural reforms need to be undertaken. A boost in production should be encouraged not merely through announcement of the policies, but by having a well-orchestrated programme to help many of our existing MSMEs and new entrepreneurs who are ready to take the plunge. The hi-tech science and technology (S&T) and academic institutions in the country like DAE (Department of Atomic Energy), DRDO (Defence Research and Development Organisation), ISRO, CSIR (Council of Scientific and Industrial Research), CMTI (Central Manufacturing Technology Insitute), IITs, NITs (National Institutes of Technology), and the like, should be mandated to help them through various forms of knowledge and skill generation.

- In doing all of the above facilitation for the industries, especially the MSMEs, great care needs to be taken regarding intellectual property rights (IPRs) and other provisions of the WTO. Otherwise, even for domestic production, we may face problems.

- In all the schools, colleges, scientific and technological institutions, the slogan for the youth, alongside 'Reinforce Agriculture—we will be the best in the world' should be 'Manufacturing will be the new frontier of India's success'. Young persons have to think on these lines instead of aspiring only to be a part of the IT industry as a low-value contributor.

- Most of the existing workforce needs to reskilled for modern, highly competitive, high-quality, low-cost manufacturing.

If all this is done in right earnest, India will make a mark in the world manufacturing business, and as a result millions of young, middle-aged and elderly Indians will get stable, better-earning jobs. That is the scope of the manufacturing sector in India, if it is tied up properly with the agriculture sector, diverse domestic needs and the global markets.

5 Mining
Adding Value to Our Natural Resources

Nature gives us its bounties both above the surface and beneath the earth. We all know about the gifts of nature that are found above—the plants that give us vital foods, herbs that we derive medicines from, fibers like cotton from which we make clothing, trees from which we derive a whole range of products, and so on. Water resources make life itself possible. Above all, the shining sun is the greatest source of energy. We know instinctively how closely all these are interconnected.

The gifts of nature that are above the earth are also interconnected with those that are found below the surface. The most obvious of the assets below the earth is groundwater, on which most of us survive nowadays. The roots of trees draw nutrition from below the soil. And most of the power that we use to run all kinds of appliances is generated from the fuels that are buried deep inside the ground—coal and natural gas.

Another material required in large quantities for modern life is iron, which we mostly use as steel. Iron is a natural resource too, just like other metals like copper and aluminum and the rare earth materials which are all vital to human civilization. In fact, human civilization progressed from the early agricultural stage when man discovered metals, which enabled him to make tools. It was through mining that humans sustained themselves, as civilization became more sophisticated. Mining continues to be important even now; it is a vital sector of the economy, and a large number of Indians are employed productively in this sector.

In *India 2020* we had elaborated on the history of mining in India. After Independence, some efforts were made to liberate the sector from the shackles of earlier monopolistic controls through nationalization. The government since then tried to take steps to make mining a vital economic growth story. But the steps were halting and the cancer of corruption also entered into the sector. In addition, environmental activism and uncertainty about the use of coal further slowed the growth down.

Mining in India

The metal and mining industry in India was estimated at around US$106.4 billion in 2010. The mining industry's contribution to the GDP varies between 2.25 and 2.5 per cent. However, if we look at only the industrial sector (to which it belongs), mining constitutes about 10 to 11 per cent of the sector. It productively employs about 700,000 persons.[1] Therefore, when mines are closed in India for one reason or another, the lives of 700,000 people as well as their families are affected. In fact, there is scope for Indian mines to grow much more. Instead of merely mining minerals and exporting them, Indian companies can make a number of value additions in the chain, creating more wealth and therefore more employment and better incomes for a significant number of Indians.

As per an Ernst & Young (E&Y) report, India currently produces around eighty-nine minerals under various groups, namely, fuel minerals, metallic minerals, non-metallic minerals, atomic minerals and minor minerals. The report says that 'the country has immense potential for mining resources and reserves and is currently among the top 10 global producers of many minerals'.[2]

TABLE 5.1 India's global position in mineral production

Mineral	Global Rank
Coal	3
Chromite	3
Iron Ore	4
Bauxite (for Aluminium)	6
Manganese Ore	5

Source: Annual Report, Ministry of Mines, FY 2013

Around the globe the mining industry was growing at a rapid pace for over a decade till 2008–09 when the global recession hit the demand. Indian mining was also affected. In addition, India had other problems. The E&Y report says: 'After growing at more than 8 per cent for many years, the Indian economy registered a GDP growth of 5 per cent in FY 13. The ongoing slowdown had an impact on demand for metals across all the major consuming sectors.' Thus the mineral production registered a negative growth.

At the same time, the court order banning iron ore mining in the states of Karnataka and Goa (recently lifted) caused an additional slowdown. Other similar court orders and government actions led to a near-complete stoppage of coal mining in India. India, which has rich coal reserves, now had to import coal.

These two elements caused severe balance-of-payment problems. According to recent reports, the demand–supply gap for coal is likely to reach 185 million tonnes by the end of 2017 if things remain as they are now.

Some Details on Mines

The total number of mines in India is more than 3100, including more than 550 fuel mines, more than 560 metal mines and over 1700 extractive non-metal mines.[3] The net production of selected minerals in 2005–06 were as in Table 5.2 below.

A similar table (Table 5.3) shows the export of select minerals in 2004–05.

It is surprising to learn that India's natural sources are not fully assessed as yet. A number of areas are still unexplored and mineral resources of these areas are yet to be assessed. While space-based remote sensing can be of help to some extent here, actual ground surveys are also required. Mountain ranges and forested areas need to be surveyed; in addition, Indian's marine territory is still relatively underexplored (the only exploration has been for natural gas).

TABLE 5.2 Net Production of Selected Minerals in 2005–06

Mineral	Quantity	Unit	Mineral Type
Coal	403	Million tonnes	Fuel
Lignite	29	Million tonnes	Fuel
Natural Gas	31,007	Million cubic metres	Fuel
Crude Petroleum	32	Million tonnes	Fuel
Bauxite	11,278	Thousand tonnes	Metallic Minerals
Copper	125	Thousand tonnes	Metallic Minerals
Gold	3,048	Thousand grams	Metallic Minerals
Iron Ore	140,131	Thousand tonnes	Metallic Minerals
Lead	93	Thousand tonnes	Metallic Minerals
Manganese Ore	1,963	Thousand tonnes	Metallic Minerals
Zinc	862	Thousand tonnes	Metallic Minerals
Diamond	60,155	Carats	Non-Metallic Minerals
Gypsum	3,651	Thousand tonnes	Non-Metallic Minerals
Limestone	170	Million tonnes	Non-Metallic Minerals
Phosphorite	1,383	Thousand tonnes	Non-Metallic Minerals

Source: Ministry of Mines, cited in Wikipedia.

TABLE 5.3 Export of Select Minerals from India in 2004–05

Mineral	Quantity Exported in 2004–05	Unit
Aluminium	896,518	Tonnes
Bauxite	1,131,472	Tonnes
Coal	1,374	Tonnes
Copper	18,990	Tonnes
Gypsum and plaster	103, 003	Tonnes
Iron Ore	83, 165	Tonnes
Lead	81,157	Tonnes
Limestone	343,814	Tonnes
Manganese Ore	317,787	Tonnes
Marble	234,455	Tonnes
Mica	97,842	Tonnes
Natural Gas	29,523	Tonnes
Sulphur	2,465	Tonnes
Zinc	180,704	Tonnes

Source: Ministry of Mines, cited in Wikipedia.

What Are the Impediments?

The biggest problem perhaps is the mindset towards mining. While most educated Indians show an interest (from afar) in agriculture, which they consider vital for the country, mining immediately throws up a visual image of a dark, damp and dirty world. How many of us have ever been to a mine, in the way that we have visited farmlands, dams and dairy farms?

The government too has largely ignored mines. The Mines and Minerals (Development and Regulation) Act (MMDRA) enacted in 1957 gave the ownership to the minerals in all the mines in India (even those which were under private ownership) to the state governments. The state governments collected rent and fees from the mines as per the provisions of the MMDRA. The revenues thus collected went to the consolidated funds of the concerned state government, to be used at the government's discretion for any expenditure in the state. As it happened, very little of this money was put back into the mining industry. Little attention was given to the improvement of technology and management in the mines or to the working conditions of the mine workers, their safety, the welfare of their families, the development of the local community or the improvement of local environments which are naturally affected by mining operations. Very slow induction of technologies led to further inefficiencies and wastages which affected the local environment and the health of local communities.

Such apathy over decades led to mining virtually vanishing from the popular mindset.

Even after economic liberation in the early 1990s, little attention was given to economic and industrial reforms in this sector. The public sector still dominated mining, with most mines working in the same slow phase. A dynamism had to be injected into mining—how was this to be done?

When privatization of some of the coal and iron ore mines was attempted during the 1990s and later during the 2000s, in principle it was a very positive move. The big monolithic public sector mining units had become obsolete technologically and were unwieldy to manage. Therefore, some competition from the private sector could make a significant difference, with higher production targets, more efficiency in terms of inputs and outputs, better cost controls, and so on. While part of this goal was achieved, the process of allotting mines led to several questions, pointing to favouritsm, and resulting in huge losses to the government exchequer. These led to public outrage. The courts ordered cancellations of many allotments, closure of some mines, and so on.

We had emphasized in *India 2020* that mines in India should not just be in a 'dig-transport-export-earn-profit' mode. If value addition is done, the ore wealth can multiply many times over; it can also create better incomes and employment for the locals. As a result, India's GDP would grow faster.

Unfortunately, India's government systems—both Central and state—as well as the private and public sector industries are short-term-oriented. They look at small gains to be made in the 'quarters' of a year and ignore long-term losses. This attitude of 'let us cross the bridge when we come to it' has led to severe losses to the country and its people, not just in mining but in other sectors as well. This same short-sighted approach leads to a lack of improvements in infrastructure and supply-chain logistics, and problems with environmental clearances.

A recent (May 2014) report by the coal ministry to the government emphasized three elements that need immediate action:

- Critical rail links for evacuation of coal from the mines directly to the customers;
- Quicker environmental clearances; and
- Speedy development of captive coal blocks, that is, those coal mines that are dedicated to one consumer such as a steel company.

Addressing these issues of mining would mean formulating an action plan that should show very quick results.

The list of impediments to the growth of the mining sector that we have looked at is not exhaustive, but it points to the critical elements that are holding up mining. The country's ability to quickly solve these and move ahead fast will decide how India will use its mineral resources and the resulting growth in GDP and spurt in employment that it will see. It is certainly not the job of the prime minister or the Central government alone; but they can set the pace. What we really need is a change in our mindset about mining.

What Are the Steps Ahead?

A number of suggestions have been made about the immediate actions required to bring the mining sector back on track and put it on a rapid growth path. There are reports by the Confederation of Indian Industries (CII), several consultants' reports, and also analytical reports in business newspapers. Drawing on these and based on our own studies, here is our action plan for mining:

- Give a special status to the mining sector (including for value additions therein) as it is critical for the economy. The idea should be to facilitate projects and fast-forward approvals, and not to create more bureaucratic hurdles.
- Fine-tune the existing MMDR Act and the procedures resulting from it so that mining sector growth can be sped up, with reduced delays in permits, clearances, and so on, and also create a sense of confidence in the sector.
- As India's mineral wealth is still not fully explored, increase efforts for surveys, pre-exploration studies and actual explorations to utilize the potential reserve. The government may do some of this and also incentivize private players, both Indian and foreign, to step up, perhaps giving them special concessions to be the first ones to use part of the ore for their commercial purposes.
- Take immediate action to retrieve all the cases that are under litigation and held up as a result of past actions. They should be studied and provided a one-time solution, agreed on by the Central and state governments, the judiciary and concerned bodies like the CAG (Comptroller and Auditor General). Many cases have been delayed for several years

and Indian mining has nearly come to a grinding halt as a result, affecting the economy and the lives of millions of Indians. We need to move forward urgently.

- In the above process some fines may be levied for fast action. Also in new auctions and allotments payments will be received by the government. These must not be diverted to the consolidated fund of state governments but should be set aside to be used for improvements in the mining sector.

- When all this begins to yield results, with more mines opening and starting production, the biggest current bottleneck, namely the capacity to extract ore from the mines quickly and reach consumers speedily, will become even more of an issue. This is crucial especially for coal and iron ore. Cost-effective mineral transportation systems must be planned right now, and implemented soon.

- As pointed out earlier, the mining sector lacks modern technologies for efficient production, reduction of pollution and workers' safety. These need to be attended to on a priority basis.

- Closely coupled with the above is the need to reskill the existing workforce and adequately skill new entrants to the sector. Companies, after making increased investments in the mining sector, should not have to complain about human resources.

- All the above are oriented towards production, efficiency, environmental cleanness, technology, safety, and so on, inside the mines. Of course these are vital. But beyond the mines are the people living around the mining areas. Do we care for them? Most companies and government agencies do have welfare schemes for their employees, but the fact is that there are many more people living around the mines who are not employed in the mines. They have lived there for generations and are no longer carried away by slogans of mines being 'temples of modern India'. They have seen the neglect of the mining sector over six decades and have suffered as a result. It is essential that these people are also taken care of when we think of reviving and accelerating the growth of mines. If value-addition activities are encouraged around the mines, instead of mere digging and transporting, many local people will get better-paying jobs.

- Until we reach an ideal scenario where mines are powered by clean sources, it is essential to locate thermal power plants close to coal mines. This will result in an improved economy and employment for the neighbourhood.

These action points need to be taken up not one at a time but all at once—the situation in our mining industry needs to be addressed urgently. The time to make the change is now. To quote Kabir, *'Kal karey so aaj kar, aaj karey so ab'*—what you would do tomorrow, you must do today; what you would do today, do right now!

6 Infrastructure
The Blood, Bones and
Muscles of the Economy

We have so far covered, in some detail, the core sectors of the economy: agriculture and mining, which reap the harvests of natural resources, and the human ingenuity of manufacturing, which converts and shapes primary materials into useful products.

It would not be possible for any of these three sectors to grow in isolated pockets. Today, India faces huge infrastructural challenges. The rapid economic growth post-liberalization has placed huge demands on the transportation systems for both goods and passengers. Domestic travel—for business, pleasure or tourism—has grown manifold. Rapid urbanization and the fast growth of the metros have also placed a heavy load on traffic.

As it happens often in India, policymakers and administrators have not kept up with the rapid growth, and the existing infrastructure is creaking under the weight of a rapidly modernizing nation. It is important to remember that the body of the economy is supported by the bones, muscles and blood of infrastructure—systems that carry millions of tonnes of goods and millions of passengers to and fro. Without an adequate infrastructural setup, a nation cannot grow beyond a point.

The Technology Vision 2020 exercise had addressed the development of India's road transport, waterways, and so on, in great detail. The only part of the recommendations which was implemented was the building of the Golden Quadrilateral, linking the cities of Delhi, Mumbai, Chennai and Kolkata, and a north–south–east–west corridor connecting Kanyakumari to Srinagar and Silchar to Porbandar.

Let us quickly survey the different segments of infrastructure in India.

Roads

India has the second largest road network in the world, covering about 4.7 million km. But not all of the roads are of the same size and quality.

- National Highways (NH) form about 1.7 per cent of the total, that is, about 79,116 km.

- State highways (SH) form about 3.3 per cent of the total, which is about 155,716 km.
- District and rural roads (DRR) form the bulk (95 per cent) with about 44,45,010 km.[1]

As anyone who travels in India will know, most of the rural and district roads and major parts of the state highways need big improvements. If they had been in better shape, the problem of food inflation would not have been as severe as it is. A good percentage of farm products, particularly perishable vegetables and fruits, don't reach the markets at all because of inadequate road systems. In some places the wastage is close to 30 per cent. The consumer suffers as a result, and the farmer is badly hit. This shows how crucial infrastructure is to the economy. The state and national highways are also vital bones and muscles for the mining and manufacturing sectors.

The alternative mode of transport is the railways and to a lesser extent the waterways. For environmental considerations, railways and waterways consume less energy per unit of freight carried than roadways, so these would in fact be the preferred mode of transport in a modern economy. But even though the railways carry a lot of traffic, the fact is that they have not kept pace with the growing demands of the economy and society. The development of waterways has been stagnant for years. Therefore the brunt is faced by road transport: it carries about 85 per cent of the passenger traffic and 60 per cent of the freight. Many private carriers find it convenient to use even the poor-quality roads. In addition, road transport is flexible in terms of the place of origin, the route and destination.

A recent report shows what is holding up the development of the road system in India:

> After awarding 6,491 km of roads in FY 12, the road sector witnessed a slump in award of projects with only 1,156 km road projects being bid by NHAI in FY 13, which is about 17 per cent of the target of 7,000 km set for the financial year. This lower than projected awards have been on account of weak interest from private sector participants due to difficulty in raising funds, stressed financial position of many developers, delays in getting the right of way and clearances, relatively less lucrative stretches in the offering, as well as the economic slowdown.[2]

This is the state of affairs with regard to the NH system, which is key to the economy and only a small part of the entire road system. Recently, the government has announced a plan for NH road construction to reach a level of completion of about 23 km per day, from the current level of 2 km per day.

It is not that the problems given in the ICRA report are unknown to the government. The report of the ministry of road transport and highways, Outcome Budget 2013–14 summarizes the problems of underperformance:

A comprehensive review reveals that there has been shortfall in the achievements of the targets due to delay in land acquistion, environmental clearances, road overbridge clearances, law and order problems, rehabilitation and settlement issues, and in some cases due to poor performance by the contractors.

What is required is a strong political will and an efficient management structure to build confidence for developers and investors and for officials to perform at their optimum capacity. In addition, a strong Centre–state collaboration is a must, especially for the development of rural roads. The national and state highways are of course priorities, but rural roads are equally important. In a body, it is not enough if the arteries and veins work well. If capillary distribution is not good, most parts of the body will not receive blood. Rural roads are like the capillary blood vessels.

It is in this context that the PURA (Providing Urban Facilities in Rural Areas) concept that Dr Kalam has advocated for over one and a half decades becomes essential. The core of PURA is physical connectivity, with rural roads connecting to nearby state or national highways or a railway station.

A Novel Suggestion for Road Projects

None of the government documents on road projects that we have seen address the need for trained human resources. They are focused instead on the narrow Five Year Plan targets or even Financial Year targets. The aspirations of Indians today are much higher. They want India to move at a fast pace. They are fed up with hearing excuses for underperformance and promises of future performance. They want to see things happening *now*.

With these aspirations in mind, we need to increase the targets for road projects. These are the targets we suggest:

National Highways	50 km per day
State Highways	100 km per day
Rural Roads	1000 km per day

Are these targets achievable? Yes, if we jettison the traditional method of only using persons from the Central and state government agencies to supervise, survey, test and carry out the work. A large workforce will have to be created and deployed for this important mission. The resultant employment generation will be seen throughout the country.

Why don't we use the young undergraduate and graduate students in the 40,000-odd colleges spread across India, especially those from the 10,000 engineering and professional colleges? They can be easily trained to do the paperwork required. They could be given small stipends and, importantly, certificates of work.

Similarly, the government subsidy schemes for employment or poverty alleviation or food security could be tied to road projects; this would in fact provide employment to millions of Indians in road-making and road repair projects; subsidies would not even be required.

Also, since the average age of Indians has gone up, we could utilize many of the retired persons to supervise, test and to do a large part of the paperwork and computer work for performance monitoring.

We must remember that we have to approach the road projects with a new impetus and great urgency. We have three decades of backlog to catch up on in road construction, and several old roads and bridges needing immediate repair and maintenance. We thus need all the human resources we can muster: unskilled and semi-skilled, students and workers, and senior citizens in addition to the usual workforce we deploy now from government agencies and private contractors.

To monitor the progress of the work, it is possible to use space technology in the form of high-resolution satellite imagery as well as GPS (Global Positioning Data).

In fact, in most of the documents on roadways very little is said about technology. Even the ministry document on roadways only makes a cursory reference to R&D (with budgets around a princely sum of Rs 2 crore). But technology should not be neglected for too long. While it is difficult to get into the technologies of the big equipment and machinery required for road construction right away, it may be useful to concentrate on the technology for equipment for regular maintenance and small-scale repairs of rural roads.

Railways

Historically speaking, the railways built by the British—albeit for their own purposes—brought the idea of 'one India' home to most Indians. After Independence, continuous improvements have been made to Indian Railways. Several metre gauge train tracks have been made broad gauge, steam engines have been replaced by diesel engines and electrical locomotives. Still, there are a number of regions in India, like the north-east and some parts of interior India, which are as yet uncovered by the railway network.

Here are some recent vital statistics about the railways in India:

- Total route network of 64,600 km
- 29.98 per cent of the network is double-track or multi-track
- A total of 7146 railway stations
- Indian Railways operates 19,000 trains every day
- Recently, Jammu and Kashmir has come on the railway map
- It owns 239,321 wagons, 61,899 coaches and 9549 locomotives
- Its total assets in 2012–13 were worth US$53.8 billion

- It operated about 12,355 passenger trains during FY 2012–13 carrying about 30 million passengers on a daily basis
- About 975.2 million tonnes of freight was transported via trains in 2012–13
- About 73 per cent of Indian Railways' revenues are from the freight traffic; profits from the freight traffic subsidizes passenger traffic
- Interestingly, major freight railways abroad, such as in the USA, China and Russia, have one-fourth the freight rate compared to India.[3]

When we speak of the railways, the story of the Metro networks is interesting to study. Helmed by E. Sreedharan, the Delhi Metro has been a great success: it is an excellent example of project management and is renowned for its dependability. But it is important to remember that India's technological, industrial and manufacturing capabilities are such that most of the components for the Metro had to be imported. Interestingly, Indian Railways had designed and built a mostly indigenous Metro in Calcutta (now Kolkata) some three decades ago; but when it came to building Metros in other cities, we had to fall back on imports. Had we persisted with developing an indigenous industrial capability to build a world-class modern Metro, even as a joint venture, we would have created the base for a whole new industry for the future.

The government has taken a number of new initiatives to improve the railways. The measures include a new policy for 'participative models for rail-connectivity and capacity-augmented projects', an automobile freight train operator scheme to encourage automobile transportation through railways, and a special purpose vehicle (SPV) for two dedicated freight corridor projects serving the west and the east, with dedicated freight lines of about 3300 km.

These are steps in the right direction. But again Indian Railways (and the railways ministry) should learn from the experiences of executing NHAI projects and try to avoid the same hurdles for private sector participation in railways development. This would only slow the growth down. India today demands fast action. In keeping with this spirit, modernization is the current mantra of Indian Railways. They took positive steps in the 1980s with computerized ticketing and reservations; now they have introduced mobile booking services. But along with these the physical assets like platforms, carriages, etc., too need modernization. Traffic safety is another area of major concern.

Finally, it is important for the railways to move away from the subsidy culture and attract private investment. We need to do all that is innovative to make the railways carry an optimum amount of freight and passenger traffic safely and speedily. The parts of the country where the railways do not currently reach, for example the north-eastern states and other hilly regions, should also be covered by the railways in the foreseeable future, perhaps in a decade or so.

Ports

Ancient India was known for its world trade. Even in the nineteenth century, India had a share of about 30 per cent of world trade, next only to China. Most of this trade took place through India's seaports.

India is endowed with an extended coastline, over 7500 km long, interspersed with more than 200 ports (thirteen of which are major ports). India has a unique advantage in that most cargo ships between East Asia and America, Europe and Africa pass through Indian territorial waters. All our major ports and about 176 of the non-major ports are in strategic locations.

But as in other fields, our port authorities have not kept up with modernization, and as a result the ports are slow in operation and attract little traffic.

According to an IBEF report on ports, cargo traffic in FY 2012 was about 911.5 MMT. The target for FY 2017 is 1756 MMT. The government has initiated a National Maritime Development Policy (NMDP) to develop the maritime sector with a plan outlay of about US$11.8 billion. In addition, the government allows FDI under the automatic route and a ten-year tax holiday for enterprises engaged in ports.

These are positive measures. But resorting to business-as-usual after making lofty policy pronouncements will not suffice. A lot can be achieved through an aggressive, creative management style. A full-time team has to be made responsible at the Centre to attract projects and meet or even exceed the targets. The team should also help in getting necessary environmental clearances and local permissions for port projects.

If maritime infrastructure in the ports develops well, not only will this help the overall economy but many local persons in the coastal areas will get better-paying employment. The states which have coastal areas utilize these assets to speed up their economy with coastal wealth and their several ports.

Waterways

Inland waterways can carry high volumes of freight and passenger traffic. We had outlined some of their possibilities in *India 2020*. In fact, our recommendations were quite conservative, looking at modernizing the traditional inland waterways through proper dredging, providing lighting facilities en route and also navigation facilities. A great deal more can be done if we look at building a new inland waterways network. It should be remembered that energy consumption per unit of freight on the waterways is much less than on roads and railways.

Surprisingly, little has been done in this area in the sixteen years since our book was published in 1998.

Airports

The aviation industry in India has done remarkably well since the Vision 2020 reports. The low-cost air carriers have created a revolution of sorts, with affordable fares and dependable services leading to many travellers now using flights for both business travel and tourism. With online booking facilities, the flights are also easy to book, and travel time is far less than by any other mode of transport.

The number of airports is increasing too: the number of operational airports in 2000 was fifty; by 2012 the number had grown to 125. Many airports are getting modernized, with six airports—Delhi, Mumbai, Bangalore, Hyderabad, Chennai, Kolkata—built and run in the public–private partnership (PPP) model. Sixty per cent of airport traffic is now handled in PPP mode with the remaining 40 per cent run by the Airports Authority of India (AAI). It is a system that seems to be working reasonably well.

On the other hand, the public sector company Air India has run continuous losses over several years now and is continuing on government subsidies, in other words, on taxpayers' money. That money could be spent better in improving critical parts of aviation infrastructure in India, for example, in building 100-seater passenger jets. There is a case for liberalizing the aviation sector further, starting with a new management style in Air India, and also allowing more foreign investment into the sector, both in airports and air services. This would help tourism grow and provide jobs for many skilled and unskilled workers, boosting the economy.

The Way Ahead

There is a lot that needs to be done for infrastructure. We must remember that without an adequate infrastructure, our economy cannot truly flourish. Why don't we designate the next ten-odd years, 2015–25, as the 'Infrastructure Decade', at the end of which the current unhappy conditions of the roads, railways, ports, etc., will be a thing of the past?

7 Biodiversity
Balancing Commerce and Conservation

Ever since life appeared on the planet about 3.7 million years ago, many species have appeared and subsequently become extinct. Some estimates are that only about 1 to 3 per cent of the species that have ever been on earth now survive.[1] The issue before us now is how to conserve them. An important part of this is to understand what the particular use of a species is. Human tendency is to not care for things which are not beneficial or useful to them. It is thus crucial to appreciate why a variety of species exist, how they are connected to each other and to a larger bio-system, and what use they are to mankind. This is what the study of biodiversity is all about.

There is a great deal of research which indicates that the conservation of biodiversity is in the long-term interest of the ecology of the earth and therefore the survival of human beings. It might be difficult, however, for many an individual to fully comprehend this. It thus becomes an issue of public good that must be taken care of by the government, with taxpayers' money being used for the cause. But there are limits to taxation; therefore, one of the ways to ensure the conservation of biodiversity is to derive some commercial benefits out of some of the diverse biological organisms. This ensures public support, as we have seen with the preservation and propagation of medical plants, aromatic herbs, and the like, whose beneficial uses are now established.

Based on the current information we have, our assumption is that terrestrial biodiversity is about twenty-five times greater than marine biodiversity. But this view may change as we explore oceans more. Also as organisms underneath the soil are studied more as part of the new field of soil biology, we may discover many more species. On an average, up to 10,000 new species (many of them insects) are discovered each year. Many that are discovered are yet to be classified. As per our current knowledge, the number of species on land and in the oceans can be seen from Table 7.1.

TABLE 7.1 Discovered and Predicted Total Number of Species on Land and in the Oceans

Species	Earth				Ocean			
	Catalogued	Predicted	± SE		Catalogued	Predicted	±SE	
Eukaryotes								
Animalia	953,434	7,770,000	958,000		171,082	2,150,000	145,000	
Chromista	13,033	27,500	30,500		4,859	7,400	9,640	
Fungi	43,271	611,000	297,000		1,097	5,320	11,100	
Plantae	215,644	298,000	8,200		8,600	16,600	9,130	
Protozoa	8,118	36,400	6,690		8,118	36,400	6,690	
Total	1,233,500	8,740,000	1,300,000		193,756	2,210,000	182,000	
Prokaryotes								
Archaea	502	455	160		1	1	0	
Bacteria	10,358	9,680	3,470		652	1,320	436	
Total	10,860	10,100	3,630		653	1,320	436	
Grand Total	1,244,360	8,750,000	1,300,000		194,409	2,210,000	182,000	

SE = Standard Error
Source: Wikipedia.

Biodiversity in India

A chapter in the Environment Audit Report[2] provides some important information about biodiversity in India. The report starts with this summary statement:

India is one of the 17 identified mega biodiverse countries of the world. With only 2.4 per cent of the total land area of the world, the known biodiversity of India contributes 8 per cent to the known global biodiversity.

This is certainly a matter of great pride to any Indian. But the report goes on to say:

It has been estimated that at least 10 per cent of the country's recorded wild flora and the same percentage of its wild fauna are on the threatened list, many of them on the verge of extinction.

The report provides key information about the different species existing in India (Table 7.2).

The audit report also lists the threats to biodiversity in India. These are:

- Nearly 74 per cent of India's population substantially depends on biodiversity resources for fodder, fuel wood, timber, etc.

- Due to increased population the land–to–man ratio and the forest–to–man ratio have rapidly declined.
- This leads to human encroachments on forested areas and unsustainable extractions.
- Unsound development strategies are also a threat.[3]

We do of course have a number of laws pertaining to biodiversity and its protection. India is a party to the Convention on Biological Diversity (CBD) since 1984. As a result of this association, the Biological Diversity Act (BDA) was enacted in 2002. As provided in the BDA, a National Biodiversity Authority (NBA), located in Chennai, was established by the Government of India in 2003. The NBA comes under the ministry of environment and forests.

TABLE 7.2   Species in India

Species	Number
Plants	455,500
Animals	91,000
Insects	59,553
Fish	2,546
Amphibians	240
Reptiles	460
Birds	1,232
Mammals	397

The activities of the NBA are by and large a slow story of forming expert committees which work for a few years, then dwindle away without having provided an action plan. Many state governments do not have corresponding state biodiversity authorities (SBAs). There is no central database. Issues related to IPRs, which are important when it comes to commercialization of biodiversity, are neglected. As a result, Indian researchers are unable to file for patents without the correct guidelines and lose out in international corporation agreements. The ministry of environment and forests of course has many other issues and problems to attend to, but as a result biodiversity loses out on the attention it deserves.

What Next?

The problems facing biodiversity are serious and we do not have any easy solutions to offer. This need is immediate and overwhelming, and it requires rapid and effective extraction and utilization of India's rich natural and mineral resources. But much of these resources are in forested, biodiversity-rich areas, and it is virtually impossible to extract them without affecting the biosphere. It is a genuine dilemma, and we need to tread cautiously.

What is needed is proper knowledge of biodiversity, a recognition of the practical needs of the local people and the economic needs of the nation, an engagement with better engineering practices to minimize disturbances to biodiversity and, above all, calm, unbiased, collective decision-making on the best ways to proceed. It is difficult to come up with practical solutions that apply to all of biodiverse India. The approach should be to focus on a few specific areas initially, which can then form a blueprint for larger action. We are confident that if India's best brains make a sincere attempt, we can strike the perfect balance between conservation and commerce.

8 The Chemistry of Life

Most materials of common or daily usage come from the chemicals industry: these include textiles, paper, paint, varnish, leather, plastics, soaps, perfumes, cleaning materials, personal hygiene products, etc. On a larger scale, many industrial products like derivatives of coal, gas, petroleum, etc., as well as fertilizers and pesticides come from the use of chemical engineering. Sometimes we don't realize how essential chemicals are to a product like a car or a computer: the paint, seats, tyres or battery of a car all use chemicals. For textiles or woodworks, chemicals are used at every stage of production.

Some people tend to automatically associate the chemicals industry with pollution. The truth is that even pollution mitigation and waste management are done by a chemical process. The advances in chemical technology and engineering are now leading to many processes which are clean, unlike in the past. Before approving any factory or chemical industry, it is essential to lay down procedures for a surrounding clean environment through technological and natural processes.

The chemicals industry is one of the oldest in India. It occupies the sixth position worldwide, and ranks third in Asia. This is good to see, but in the modern competitive world, one cannot rest on past laurels or be complacent about the present. Innovations are taking place constantly in technology, in business models and in customer services. Newer chemical standards for purity and safety are being established all the time. Most pesticides that were widely used worldwide fifty years ago are now considered toxic. Products like leather which use azo dyes cannot be sold when the residues are only in parts per million (ppm) level. Some countries are also adopting different business models to sell better chemicals at cheaper price points.

Overview of the Indian Chemicals Industry

As per a TIFAC–Indian Chemical Council (ICC) report of January 2014, to which we will refer extensively, there are about 40,000 chemical manufacturing units in India, of which 80 per cent are in the small–scale sector. This industry as a whole produces nearly 70,000 types of commercial products over a wide range of categories ranging from cosmetics and toiletries to plastics and pesticides. There are about 3.3 million people employed in the sector.[1]

As per the report, the chemicals can be categorized into three broad areas:

Basic Chemicals   53 per cent
Knowledge Chemicals   29 per cent
Speciality Chemicals   18 per cent

The total production value for basic chemicals is about US$57 billion. Basic chemicals are further classified in four levels. Organic and inorganic chemicals have a market share of 10 per cent, while fertilizers and petrochemicals have a market share of 90 per cent.

One important point that is emphasized in the TIFAC report is that the chemical industry by its very nature is energy intensive in the manufacturing processes and also in terms of the use of raw material: it draws on the same sources like gas, oil, coal, etc., both as raw material for products and also as energy sources for the manufacturing process. Therefore, one continual action for competitiveness in this sector is to strive for better energy efficiency. In addition, the government should create enabling mechanisms to provide access to cheaper energy sources specifically for the chemicals industry.

The report is full of data comparing the energy efficiencies of various sectors of chemical production in India. We will give one example from the fertilizer industry (Table 8.1) which shows how energy efficiency has increased over the decades.

TABLE 8.1   Energy Consumption
Trend in an Average Indian Ammonia
Plant, 1987–88 to 2009–10

1987–88	12.48
1997–98[2]	11.00
2009–10	8.78

Unit of energy consumption: gigacalories per metric tonne (GCal/MT)
World benchmark is 6.78, some individual plants are at around 7.70.

Key Recommendations for the Basic Chemical Sector in India

Again, we will draw upon the TIFAC–ICC report which makes some excellent recommendations.

1. Firstly, the industry should look for feed stocks alternate to the current modes of crude oil and natural gas. Indian reserves in these are low. Alternative processes with suitable technology are available for coal, biomass and possibly shale oil (of which India has estimated reserves between 8.50 trillion and 59.44 trillion cubic metres).

2. We import PVC, acrylic acid, phenol and methanol in large quantities. The government should provide stimulating policies to encourage entrepreneurs to invest in plants for these in India.

3. The domestic feed stock supply can be enhanced considerably by ensuring adoption of the Consortium Cracker Approach. Every petroleum, chemicals and petrochemicals investment region, which has specialized SEZs (special economic zones) dedicated to the chemicals industry, must have a naptha cracker which produces all the building blocks such as ethylene and propylene. Such crackers can be set up by the government or in PPP mode as a consortium. This consortium could offer the necessary building blocks to promoters interested in setting up downstream petrochemicals industries. This will considerably

enhance value addition and also the production of such high-value chemicals in India. Currently manufacturers desirous of such production have to depend on imports with their attendant problems.

4. Shale gas needs urgent attention, even as we step up coal-related activities in a major way. We must not waste any time in starting shale gas exploration and production.

5. Methanol to Gasoline (MTG) is fully compatible with conventional refinery gasoline. This route needs to be pursued actively and speedily.

6. Most Indian fertilizer plants are more than fifteen years old. These aged units bring down the average energy efficiency. There are many cost-effective technologies available now. The old units may be retro-fitted, repaired and upgraded; some may have to be closed down. This should be a mission as it will help not only the competitiveness of the chemicals industry globally but also help farmers by lowering their input costs over time.

7. As we pointed out in an earlier chapter, exploration for minerals has not been carried out extensively in India. If this is done, many new rich sources may become available, around which many chemical industries can grow.

8. Focused R&D to improve competitiveness is the need of the hour. It has to be undertaken by the chemicals industry itself, as the current method of relying on the national laboratories has not yielded good and speedy results. The R&D may be done in an industry-driven consortium mode with the government providing substantial seed money initially and smaller project grants later for items which are related to 'public good'. Global laboratory practices (GLP) may also be researched and the knowledge disseminated.

9. Safety aspects of the workers and plants are extremely important. Here again, an industry-driven consortium-mode institute may be established with government grants to assist plants to develop safety systems and for retraining the existing workforce.

10. In addition, at the policy level, well-executed short-term and medium-term plans are required to address the critical concerns articulated in the TIFAC ICC report, which are as follows:

The key concerns of the Indian Chemical Industry are the small capacity of plants, higher input costs of raw materials, power, fuel, etc., and lack of world class infrastructure specially roads, ports and power supply, lack of competitiveness, cost disadvantage and also stringent labour laws. A major concern is also the various free trade agreements, which India is signing with various countries and which are aimed at phasing out trade barriers. The Industry feels unless the labour laws, power supply and infrastructure are improved, it would be very difficult to compete globally with rapidly declining duty differentials and appreciation in the value of the rupee.

11. We should also try to catch up on green chemistry and process intensification technologies and then take a leadership role in the production of IPR and actual products. These may dominate the chemicals industry in a decade or two from now.

Knowledge Chemicals

These derive their name from the higher degree of new knowledge domains involved in producing such chemicals. They include chemicals used in the pharmaceuticals, biotechnology and agro-chemical sectors. All of these are vital areas both for India and the world. India has developed an edge on a global scale in high-quality pharmaceutical manufacturing. Another TIFAC–ICC study surveys the Indian pharmaceutical industry in detail, and compares it to some of the global leaders: the USA, the EU countries, Japan and China.[3]

According to the report, the global pharmaceutical industry is estimated at US$858 trillion (in 2010) with an annual growth of about 4.5 per cent. The USA, EU and Japan consume a large percentage of the products (80 per cent in value). The higher growth would thus be in Asia (except Japan which is already a huge consumer), Latin America, Australia and Africa with a likely annual growth rate of 11 to 14 per cent.

TABLE 8.2 Top 10 Global Pharmaceutical Companies in Terms of Sales in 2010

Company	Sales in 2010 in US$ million	Share of the Global Market
Pfizer	55,602	6.5%
Novartis	46,806	5.5%
Merck & Co.	38,468	4.5%
Sanofi-Aventis	35,875	4.2%
Astrazeneca	35,535	4.1%
GlaxoSmithkline	33,664	3.9%
Roche	32,693	3.8%
Johnson & Johnson	26,773	3.1%
Abbott	23,833	2.8%
Lilly	22,113	2.6%

Source: IMS Health Midas, December 2010

The top ten companies in the world account for around 41 per cent of pharma sales.

Biotechnologically produced drugs, known as biopharmaceuticals or biologics, have been the major driver of growth for the global pharma market. The report adds that global sales of biopharma products generated US$80 billion in revenues for the companies in 2009 (that is about 10 per cent of the total pharma sales quoted before). There are about 174 products being sold worldwide. The USA itself consumes about $60 billion worth of this.

The key characteristics of the pharma industry are:

- High knowledge base and intensity
- Capital intensity
- Long cycle time for a product to reach the market due to various safety-related tests and regulatory regimes
- High uncertainty of R&D outcomes

Together, these factors make it difficult for a developing country to acquire leadership in the market. The amounts spent on R&D resulting in a successful drug (a great deal of R&D does not result in a marketable drug) are getting higher all the time. Therefore the number of breakthrough technologies are diminishing despite high spends on R&D.

A number of generic drugs have emerged instead. These are biologically equivalent to the original branded innovative drug. To give a cost and time comparison, it takes seven to ten years and over US$1 billion to develop an innovative drug and patent it; further stages of tests and more spends are required before it can be brought to the market. But a generic drug, which is essentially a good copy of the original made with different processes, takes only two to three years to develop at a much lower cost. Before the patent regimes of the WTO came into full force with an amendment to the Indian Patent Act in 2005, many Indian companies built up global standards of generics. Generics have an additional advantage that they do not have to go through extensive clinical trials because the earlier innovative (patented and branded) drug has gone through these already.

An Overview of the Indian Pharma Industry

The Indian pharma industry has come a long way, being a visible player at the global level. Here are some vital statistics about the pharma industry in India:

- Annual production worth US$21.2 billion (2009–10)
- Fourteenth in the world in terms of value

- Third in the world in terms of volume of production
- India accounts for 10 per cent of global pharma production
- Composition of pharma products in India: 80 per cent indigenous formulation, of which 85 per cent is for domestic consumption
- One of the top five producers of APIs (active pharmaceutical ingredients) in the world
- Over 400 APIs are produced in India
- Largely self-sufficient in production of APIs; also supplies APIs to the global market.

Table 8.3 provides some macro-level statistics on the Indian pharma market.

It can be seen that the import share is going up, mainly because of the import of APIs from China which are 10–15 per cent cheaper than those in India. It is to be noted that this is happening for basic chemicals as well. Cost competitiveness is a crucial issue for the Indian chemicals industry when compared to China.

The structure of Indian pharma companies is:

- The world's most competitive
- Formulation drugs manufactured from 8174 manufacturing units (out of 10,563 total units)

TABLE 8.3   Indian Pharmaceutical Market
(in US$ billion)

	2006–07	2007–08	2008–09
Domestic production	10.0	12.3	12.8
Export	5.5	7.4	8.9
Import	1.3	1.6	2.0
Share of import	11.5%	11.7%	13.4%

Source: Department of Pharmaceuticals Annual Report 2009–10

- Constitutes large, medium and small companies
- Maharashtra, Gujarat, West Bengal, Telangana-Seemandhra and Tamil Nadu account for about two-thirds of the total number of manufactures
- Major focus on generics
- Faces significant competition from China

The Indian biopharma industry is estimated at US$1.8 billion (2009–10). It is growing at an annual rate of about 12 per cent. Its main products are vaccines, diagnostics and therapeutics. The Indian vaccine market is largely driven by domestic needs. It has done wonders for the Indian public health system. Domestic sales is about 60 per cent and there is also good export growth.

Other emerging areas are biosimilars; novel drug delivery systems; biopharmaceutical therapeutics; combination vaccines; contract research and manufacturing services (CRAMS); clinical trials; and herbal actives. The Indian pharma industry is active in all these areas.

Readers may be interested in knowing about the herbs exported from India.

According to the TIFAC–ICC report, 'India, having one of the richest repositories of herbal medicines with

TABLE 8.4 Herbs Exported from India

Botanical Names	Parts Used
Acorus calamus	Rhizome
Argemone Mexicana	Fruit
Curcuma amada	Rhizome
Curcuma longa	Rhizome
Curcuma aromatic	Wild turmeric
Cassia lanceolata	Leaves
Glycyrrhiza glabra	Root
Withania somnifera	Vegetable rennet
Myrica nagi	Leaf
Piper longum	Fruit
Rubia cordifolia	Madder root
Symplocos racemosa	Bark
Swertia chirata	Whole plant
Terminalia chebula	Bark and seed
Zingiber officinale	Rhizome
Wedelia calendula	Leaf and root

Source: 'Current and Future Status of Herbal Medicines', *Veterinary World*, Vol. 1, No. 11, November 2008.

almost 25,000 effective plant based formulations, has the potential to tap the growing market. A key factor that supports the growth of this industry is India's rich biodiversity.' We have looked at the importance of biodiversity in Chapter 7. The huge earnings along with employment that can be generated from herbal medicines—which in turn would create economic growth—is a great incentive to preserve our biodiversity.

Another area for development in India could be nutraceuticals, which are natural chemical compounds possessing medicinal properties. These are marketed as supplements to improve health, prevent diseases, etc. They are sold as tablets, capsules, powders, and so on.

The emerging areas in which Indian pharma industries are fortunately present to some degree are highly knowledge-intensive. They require several new skill sets and different ways of working. This will require new forms of industry–academia collaborations. Technicians and researchers alike will need to unlearn some of the work culture they are accustomed to and learn the elements of a new, globally competitive, industrial work culture. A new testing infrastructure will be needed too, which both the government and industries will need to invest in. If we can do this, India can become one of the global leaders in knowledge chemicals in about a decade.

TABLE 8.5 Classification of Nutraceutical Compounds

Based on Ingredients	Based on Medicinal Use
• Antioxidants, carotenoids	• Bone and joint health
• Dairy-based ingredients	• Cancer risk reduction
• Fibres and carbohydrates	• Cardiovascular health and diabetes
• Minerals	• Cognitive and mental function
• Nutritional lipids and oils	• Energy and endurance
• Phytochemicals, plant extracts	• Eye health
• Probiotics and prebiotics	• Immune system
• Proteins, peptides, amino acids	• Maternal and infant health
• Soy-based ingredients	• Respiratory health
• Vitamins and premixes	• Skin health
	• Weight management

Source: 'Nutraceuticals—Critical Supplement for Building a Healthy India', Ernst & Young–FICCI, September 2009.

Speciality Chemicals

The third major sector in the chemicals industry is speciality chemicals which support many other vital sectors. These speciality chemicals include water treatment chemicals, catalysts, construction chemicals, adhesives and sealants, colourants, textile chemicals, leather chemicals, paper chemicals, plastic additives, oilfield chemicals, foundry chemicals, electronics chemicals, paints and coatings, personal care ingredients, pharmaceutical excipients and food additives.

We will refer to a TIFAC–ICC study that covers the area of speciality chemicals comprehensively.[4] What is of particular relevance to us are the sections in the report on the skill gap and the technology road map.

This is what the report has to say on the skill gap:

According to inputs received during the primary survey, the industry is impacted by a skill gap in the area of practical knowledge. It has been pointed out by respondents during the primary survey that the new entrants in the industry, while they have theoretical knowledge of chemistry and other relevant subjects, often do not have adequate practical knowledge of operating laboratory equipment. Strong theoretical background coupled with adequate practical knowledge of operating machines and laboratory equipment is the need by the industry. Following are the areas which have been mentioned as areas of skill gap by the respondents during our primary survey:

- Skills to operate machines
- Knowledge of operating laboratory equipment
- Adhere to safety aspects in conducting lab work
- Knowledge of compliance to processes
- Technical knowledge of Good Laboratory Practices (GLP)

Lack of industry–academia interactions, lack of adequate infrastructure in some academic institutions and un-updated curricula have been sighted as some of the reasons for new entrants having inadequate practical knowledge. As a result, majority of the companies impart in-house technical training to the new joiners.

The TIFAC report re-emphasizes the importance of training, relearning and reskilling that we have been talking about in the context of other sectors as well.

Technology Road Map

There is a declining growth in demand in the developed markets; demand has now shifted to China, India and other emerging countries. As per the TIFAC–ICC report, escalating raw-material costs, new competition from emerging economies (regional players in the Far East, China and the Middle East) and expansion of the scope of commodity are leading to shrinking margins.

The report further states:

> In this evolving scenerio of Specialty Chemicals Industry, India offers several growth opportunities such as exports, product outsourcing hub, research outsourcing hub, etc. India's cost advantage is a key drive governing outsourcing and contract research and manufacturing services (CRAMS) in the country. Foreign companies are shifting their manufacturing base to India mainly due to a well educated pool of scientists, chemical engineers, and low labour and equipment costs. Further, multinationals are viewing smaller Indian companies as providers of their speciality chemical requirements.

The report goes on to say that:

> Emerging trends in Specialty Chemical Industry indicate a new focus on technology. New development in end-user industries such as nanotechnology, biotechnology, etc., are offering new opportunities in several areas such as electronics, food, textiles, etc.; however, success in this area demands technology

competence to develop new products and customized applications.

The report then lists the technology gaps or limitations of the Indian speciality chemical industry:

- Heavy reliance on imports
- Problems for raw materials
- Compliance to environmental regulations and guidelines
- Limited focus on research
- Limited collaboration between industry and academia.

The actions required by the government are:

- Providing financial assistance for acquiring global technology
- Attaining self-sufficiency in raw materials
- Focused research projects
- Developing herbal products for speciality applications[5]
- Developing centres of excellence for the speciality chemicals industry.[6]

Developing the sector of speciality chemicals needs to be taken up as a mission. This is an area where India can achieve a lot.

Bioproducts

These include:

- Bioethanol: ethanol from biomass, bacterial ethanol, bioconversion of cellulose, etc.
- Biochemicals: chemicals produced from biomass
- Bio-oil
- Bio-hydrogen
- Industrial enzymes for bioethanol.

These are again areas in which India can excel if we use the right technologies for agriculture, forestry, biomass production, etc. Advanced technologies will increase soil productivity, plant growth, etc., freeing up a fair amount of land from the current agricultural products like grain, fruits, vegetables, cotton, sugar cane, etc.

The Mission

The chemicals industry in India is poised for major growth if we take care of the items highlighted here. It is not without competition; China will prove to be a major competitor, and other emerging countries will make a dent in the market too. One of the major problems for India is the availability of quality, reliable, reasonably priced electricity, water and infrastructure. There will have to be an all-round upgradation; some of chemical industries that become obsolete might need to be abandoned. But those that are good and have the potential to be better need support in terms of policies, enabling infrastructure and skilled human resources. The industry, academia and government need to be speedily oriented to one mission: 'India as a chemical and biotechnology industry hub of the world'. It is something that is possible to achieve within a decade.

9 The Neural Networks of the Knowledge Economy

CHAPTER

Both of us remember the struggles ISRO went through trying to get telephone connections for its workplace and a few reliable links for the launches of its satellite and launch vehicles. Another equally difficult challenge was to procure a computer for the scientific and technical calculations. In order to get a licence to import a computer (since none were manufactured in India in those days) one had to make several trips to Delhi to meet the officials of the department of electronics. The reason for the difficulties was simple: a telephone was considered a luxury and computers were seen as anti-labour (and therefore anti-people).

For the launch of India's first satellite, *Aryabhata*, in 1975 from a launch station in a place called Kapustin Yar in the then Soviet Union, for reliable connections to the ISRO facilities in Bangalore, two sets of special telephone connections were hired from the post and telegraphs (P&T) department at a steep price. One line went along the route Bangalore–Bombay–London–Moscow, while the other followed the route Bangalore–Madras–Delhi–Moscow.

Similarly, for the 1979 launch of India's first satellite launch vehicle, SLV-3, to connect the expert team in Thumba, Trivandrum (now Thiruvananthapuram), to the launch team in Sriharikota (SHAR), ISRO had to hire a dedicated hotline at a huge price. Even then the P&T department would not allow us to be connected through the telephone exchange. At Trivandrum the experts were located on a sprawling complex of over 200 acres and in SHAR, over 36,000 acres. How could one come running to one solitary emergency phone in the facility to call the other team to solve a critical problem? It defied all logic. Yet, the P&T department applied this rule to avoid the dedicated line being used as a regular line, which would decrease the revenue they were earning. So much for customer care!

At the time of the launch of the first INSAT (Indian National Satellite System) satellite in the 1980s, the situation with telephones had become slightly better. For the country as a whole, the number of telephone lines that were laid during the fifteen years before the first Indian geosynchronous satellite, INSAT-1, became available, doubled in just eighteen months. ISRO now used direct satellite channels for its critical or emergency communications.

Gone now are the days when telephones, computers, data transfer through telephone lines, etc., were severely controlled as if they were dangerous objects. Wireless communications by individuals were banned! Even for organizations which had large-scale field activities there were many restrictions. We recall that when for the first time the prestigious international conference of the Committee on Space Research (COSPAR) was held in India in 1979 (in recognition of India's entry into space research), ISRO was not allowed to use simple low-power wireless communication for the compulsory simultaneous translation required during the inaugural session at Hotel Ashok at Bangalore. We had to resort to individual wiring of four lines for the 500-odd participants, which was cumbersome as well as costly.

Now most people in India own and use a wireless mobile phone for domestic and global communication. What a revolutionary change of mindset in less than two decades! With the slow opening up of the telephone sector during the late 1980s and the entry of the private sector during the 1990s, the Indian information and communications technology (ICT) segment burst open during the late 1990s and 2000s. This was largely thanks to the policies of the government that allowed the private sector including foreign companies entry into the segment in a major way, thus abandoning the overly centralized control by one public sector department that had existed earlier.

At the same time, there was a technology explosion worldwide: high-quality, low-loss fibre optic transmission lines became available at competitive prices; many mind-boggling developments took place in microelectronics and optoelectronics with ultra-high miniaturization and an abundance of memory space; optical CDs were made available at a very low price but with high quality. Wireless cell telephony, coupled with optical communications and satellite communications, opened up the communications sector.

The growth in the Indian telecom sector has been much more than what was envisaged during the 1995–96 TIFAC Vision studies. One of the main reasons for the rather conservative growth estimates was that none of those involved in the studies on the telecommunication sector for Technology Vision 2020 could be sure that such liberalization could take place, given that two strong government departments, the department of telecommunication (DoT) and the department of electronics (DoE), independently controlled many items connected to the ICT sector. There was meagre technological competence in the Indian industry and institutions, since this was not encouraged; there was no base for a microelectronics industry in India, which was growing by leaps and bounds in China and the Far East, not to mention the USA, Japan and Europe. It is therefore understandable that many electronic services like ATMs, etc., were highlighted in the Vision 2020 projections, but the tremendous growth these have seen was not expected.

A Giant Step Forward, But More Is Needed

India can be very proud of the rapid spread of ICT, including Internet and mobile phone connectivity and the availability of a wide range of television channels through cable TV networks and direct-to-home (DTH) satellite connections.

Internet connections were practically non-existent even twenty years ago, as the DoE was still trying to promote the low-speed ERNET (the dial-up network of the Education and Research Network), and the DoT would not allow certain data interfaces to the telephone lines. The subsequent boom has helped the youth of India to learn more, to communicate better, and to participate in the world's knowledge economy. There is a multi-billion-dollar industry in India now around ICT and TV. These in turn provide many millions of higher-income jobs to Indians.

The effects of this phenomenal growth have been far-reaching. India's talent in the modern knowledge economy, which hadn't been revealed before, caught the attention of the world. Young India awoke to new professions with exciting job profiles and better pay packages. Engineering and professional colleges came up at a rapid pace to prepare the youth with the requisite skill sets, adding to India's employable-youth pool. Meanwhile, disposable incomes in the hands of young aspirational professionals led to greater demand for and consumption of automobiles, white goods, real estate and financial services. This is a growth process that is irreversible. No Indian can dream of a rollback in ICT penetration. In fact, Indians everywhere, including in more and more rural areas, want more connectivity to mobile and Internet services, television and other forms of entertainment. Everyone wants to be connected 24×7 to the global neural network.

Let us examine the actual numbers of growth in various elements of the telecom sector. For our figures, we will draw upon the IBEF report from March 2014 on telecommunication.

Here are some vital statistics:

- With a 898 million–strong subscriber base (end 2012–13), India has the second largest telecom network in the world.
- With about 165 million Internet connections (2012), India is the third largest in the world.
- Mobile-based Internet is a key component of Indian Internet use. Seven out of eight users use a mobile phone to access the Internet.
- 'Teledensity' is the term used to define the number of telephone connections for every hundred individuals. India's teledensity was 73 per cent in 2013. The urban teledensity was 147 per cent in 2013, up from 89 per cent in 2009; the rural teledensity was 41 per cent in 2013, up from 15 per cent in 2009.

The Indian telecom market is broadly divided into three segments:

- Mobile (wireless): These provide direct communication via airwaves.

145

- Fixed line (wireline): These operate through landlines, microwaves (huge transmission towers which help in difficult terrains where laying landlines is difficult—these have been replaced now in some places by satellite communication) and a combination of satellites and landlines. The landlines we refer to here are not just the commonly seen telephone wires but also coaxial cables and fibre optic lines.

- Internet services: These draw upon the communication and transmission capabilities of the earlier two but provide broadband Internet connections through consumer and corporate channels. These businesses are described as Internet service providers (ISPs).

The wireless segment forms 96.6 per cent of total subscriptions and thus dominates the market. The rest is on wireline.[1]

The composition of telephone subscribers as of March 2013 is interesting:

- Urban Wireless   58.5 per cent
- Rural Wireless   38.1 per cent
- Urban Wireline   2.6 per cent
- Rural Wireline   0.7 per cent[2]

Mobile teledensity in India increased five times between FY 2006–07 (when it was 14.6 per cent) and FY 2012–13 (when it was 70.9 per cent).

Internet penetration has not been as fast as mobile subscriptions. There were 8.6 million Internet subscribers in India in 2006; this number increased to 25.3 million by 2012. The projected number of subscribers by 2016 is 215 million. Even among Internet subscribers, broadband subscriptions are even less: during FY 2012–13 it was 15.1 million (that is, about 60 per cent of those who have Internet access).

If Indians have to really usher in the knowledge economy, Internet services must penetrate to many more Indians. Broadband access in particular is vital, not just for business or entertainment, but also for knowledge. If broadband access is available to all Indians in the working age and at the learning stages, new skills can be imparted easily, since broadband supports good quality videos and enables interactive sessions. This is what we should aim for because it will help overcome the language divide that often holds up nationwide communication in India; simultaneous language translations are easily facilitated with broadband.

Let us hope that India will usher in the 4G revolution very soon so that such services can also be available widely on mobile phones.

According to a recent report,[3] the government is considering bringing in a new broadband policy to incentivize rollout in rural areas. As per the report, the Broadband Commission for Digital Development has estimated that India ranks 145th among the nearly 200 countries in the world in terms of percentage of individuals using the Internet, and 106th in terms of mobile penetration.

It is important to remind ourselves of these rankings and to place ourselves in a global context. While the telecom sector has made remarkable progress, a lot more needs to be done. There are still around 62,443 villages in India that are uncovered by telephone services. For many other rural areas and even some urban areas, subscribers are not too sure of the reliability of the connection. Just as reliable, quality electrical supply is the vital force for modernization, 24×7 dependable telephone connectivity and Internet access is key to the neural network that enables the growth and sustenance of the knowledge economy. This has to be made a national priority.

New Opportunities

As outlined in the IBEF report, the National Telecom Policy 2012 calls for:

- 'Broadband for all' with a minimum download speed of 2 MBps (megabytes per second)
- Increasing rural teledensity to 70 per cent by 2017 and to 100 per cent by 2020
- Liberalization of spectrum and convergence of network, services and devices
- Unified licensing, delinking of spectrum from licences, online real-time submission and processing
- Aim at a 'One Nation–One Licence' regime with no roaming charges and nationwide number portability.

We hope that the implementation of this policy will move with great speed. Two years have passed already since the policy was declared. We do not have time to waste.

If the telecom sector moves ahead as planned in the policy and the content matches up to the bandwidth, there will be a great knowledge revolution in India. This in turn would lead to economic growth.

To see how these are connected, we would like to refer to a recent report by Deloitte and CII.[4] The report quotes from the World Bank:

A 10 per cent increase in mobile and broadband penetration increases the per capita GDP by 0.81 per cent and 1.38 per cent respectively in the developing country.

Note that we are talking here not just of GDP but of per capita GDP. Enhanced mobile and broadband penetration can in fact transform the nation.

As we move on to the next chapter, we have high hopes that India's neural networks will grow even stronger in the near future and give each Indian access to the knowledge economy of the world.

10 From Waste to Wealth

The wealthier a society becomes, the more waste it produces. This is true of developing countries as well as developed ones. Even a middle-class household in the USA will have a huge refrigerator full of large cartons of juice, milk, etc. Everything from cornflakes to pizzas comes in elaborate, decorative packaging. The use of aluminum foil is very common, as is the use of 'disposable' items ranging from razors to plastic bottles of soft drinks. Needless to say, none of this is environment-friendly.

In India, cartons of milk are not that common yet, but we do use plastic packets for milk which are strewn about in the thousands after use. If you go to a conference or a high-level function, you will find a proliferation of small plastic bottles of water. And our streets—be they in cities or towns—are littered with discarded paper and plastic cups and plates, napkins, and so on.

It is a sign that in India more people are now able to afford things—people are now able to pay more to have more conveniences, and this typically includes the use of a lot of 'disposable' items. As the country develops on an economic and social register, the systems readily available for Indians to emulate are the Western ones. In some cases, we add our own twist to the array of disposable items, in the form of mini plastic cups for tea, one-time-use sachets for shampoo, small packets of mouth freshener, etc.

Western societies went through their problems of garbage disposal and waste-water challenges in the 1960s. Earlier, consumerism was rising, but the nations had not become very wealthy. Once they did, the problems with accumulated garbage cropped up. The solutions were relatively easy to find in the USA: the country has vast lands and a reasonably low population density, so they could use landfills. Europe had more problems with space and therefore started developing technologies that would convert garbage into electric power. Simple incineration was not an option as it pollutes the atmosphere. Already the coal, oil, gas and electric power stations, along with chemical and metallurgical plants, were polluting the atmosphere. There was a period in the 1960s and 1970s when Europe had to face the problems of acid rain, due to these chemicals pouring down with rainwater. Industrial emissions also polluted historical rivers like the Rhine and the Thames; large cities started having problems with smog as well.

But they moved forward and introduced cleaner technologies, capturing and eliminating particulate emissions and chemical emissions at the generating points. Of course, this needed more investments in the plants and in turn consumers had to pay higher tariffs for the power or the metals or chemicals produced, which they were prepared to do for the public good, their own welfare and the future of their progenies. In the process of conducting the necessary R&D, scientists also learned how to reduce the production of wastes in the first instance.

Moreover, these societies had inherently developed good civic discipline. Most citizens throw their wastes in prescribed trash cans both at home and in public places. There is no concept of littering. Therefore, garbage disposal or waste handling was far easier.

The results are for all to see. The Rhine and the Thames have been clean now for decades. All water bodies are maintained with a rigorous sense of cleanliness in Europe, the USA, Japan, etc. The USA is a leader in Clean Lake Management, updating the standards of cleanliness and researching into microchemical and microbiological contamination. Waste-water recycling and reuse has become part of life in most of these nations.

Beyond Waste Removal

The unprecedented growth in global business since the 1980s with an aggressive search for emerging markets in developing countries, as well as the adoption by most developing countries of a liberalized 'market economy', led to a huge growth in wealth generation. More people than ever before can now afford a good standard of living, and this means consuming more and more goods and services.

The old-style technologies were energy inefficient: they consumed large amounts of raw materials and wasted most of the intermediate products. Therefore, purely for commercial considerations, industries in the developed world started researching on and adopting energy-efficient technologies in the 1980s. These target very low levels of water or ore or other raw material consumption in chemical or metallurgical factories.

In *India 2020* we provided certain data for steel, cement making, etc., in terms of the best global achievements (till 1995) and what India should be targeting. Two decades have passed since then. For the developed world the numbers are improving year on year. While there have been some improvements with regard to energy efficiency in Indian industries, it still has a long way to go to reduce waste to measure up to global standards.

By the turn of the millennium, scientists started realizing that even the levels of global emissions of carbon dioxide were increasing dangerously. This of course is linked to the growing consumption levels of the developed and developing world. If all the people of the developing world, with its large and growing populations, realize the standards of living and consumption levels of the developed world, the planet would not be able to sustain the resultant emissions and waste. It is of course not possible to restrict consumption, as this would lead to widespread disparities and unrest.

So the solution is to go beyond merely recycling or reducing the waste. The world has to get into fundamentally new ways of engineering its products of consumption. For example, the sources of energy for transport and for electricity generation have to shift from the usual fossil fuels like coal, petroleum products and natural gas. These workhorse fuels which have helped human beings usher in the modern era will of course remain with us for at least the rest of this century. Nuclear power generation has been given a thrust by the use of uranium-based fuels. However, we would need a manifold increase in nuclear power generation even to attain a reasonable degree of energy independence. We would need to develop technologies for a wider spectrum of fissile material found around the world. For example, India has one-fourth of the world's thorium reserves. Therefore, it is essential for us to pursue the development of nuclear power using thorium. Also, nuclear fusion research needs to be progressed with international cooperation to keep that option for meeting the large power requirement at a time when fossil fuels get depleted.

In the short and medium term, India has to step up clean coal-based and gas-based electricity generation with the latest clean technologies. But simultaneously, we need to start the use of other energy sources for electricity generation. India has taken some steps to start utilizing wind and solar energy. But there are finite limitations to wind availability, and for solar energy the space required may pose limitations, as the land has other competing needs. Also, electricity generation alone cannot help the transport sector which due to the technology used still depends on fossil fuels in some form. This is where bio-based derivations like ethanol can help in a major way.

The technologies which are available now for ethanol are based on sugar cane, corn and other grains. These work very well as a blend. As we have discussed elsewhere in this book, agriculture cannot afford to waste land in inefficient ways as is too often the case in India. High-yield, low water–consumption agriculture is the need of the hour. India can feed its 1.3 billion–strong population and animals too with the use of 100 million ha of land; the rest of the arable land, about 70 million ha, can create new bio-industries of the future, producing ethanol and other cellulosic materials.

Similarly, the chemicals industry should be transformed with more and more knowledge chemicals where human intervention will make the molecular-level processes more efficient. Bioreactors may perform many processes of chemical reaction.

Solar cells may become much thinner, being just thick enough to cause the photovoltaic actions, thus saving on the silicon material, much of which currently goes waste.

Producing pure silicon requires considerable energy, which makes the wastage even more counterproductive; there is research that is ongoing in some advanced countries like Germany to try to use even relatively impure silicon blocks to generate electricity.

Materials technologies are also undergoing a major transformation with nanotechnologies and other forms of molecular coatings which will reduce material usage. Another whole new area that can become a major application is the use of algae biomass as a feed stock for biofuels. There are many more innovations that are in research stages; some of these may not work, but some will radically change the way we live.

Going forward, we need to develop a culture for using everything efficiently in terms of material consumption through the full life cycle of the product. The 'throwaway' culture of consumption needs be replaced by one of recycling. The positive effects of this will be far-reaching: it will mean a happier, more fulfilling life for the entire human population; and, as the atmosphere is slowly purged of harmful gases, marine and under-soil biology will flourish too.

All this can happen only if the idea of waste is reconceptualized, and modelled and calibrated according to scientific methods.

- It is not enough to see the chimneys of the factories not emitting black or yellow smoke; in the overall calculations of the whole value chain, the contribution of the processes to the overall increase of carbon dioxide, nitrogen, sulphur oxides and other harmful gases have to be low. This can only be calculated through scientific-engineering models of the 'footprint' of these harmful emissions.
- It is not enough to see greenery in the agricultural fields—the same calculations of footprint will be needed to look at the level of methane emissions, and so on.
- It is not enough to see blue water in the lakes and rivers; the measurement of various chemicals present in the water has to be below the specified parts per million (ppm) levels.

In order to achieve this, in the near term we have to deal with waste in its crude form and convert it into useful products under the slogan 'Waste to Wealth'. This will pave the way for the zero-waste society of the future.

Let us now look at examples of 'Waste to Wealth' that we can aim for in the short and medium term.

Solid Waste Management

There are hundreds of articles and reports on solid waste management (SWM) or municipal solid waste (MSW) in India. We will quote some numbers from a report available on the Internet[1] so that readers can see the dimensions of the issue.

As we had noted earlier, these numbers will keep increasing. We should also note that these wastes do not include night soil (human excreta) but include all other forms of garbage: biomass, animal wastes, food wastes, throwaway paper and plastic, etc. We can see that if SWM is carried out in all Class 1 cities

•	Total quantity of solid waste generated in urban areas of India (grand total)	1,15,000 tonnes per day (tpd (100%)
(a)	Waste generated in six mega cities (percentage of total)	21,100 tpd (18.35%)
(b)	Waste generated in metro cities (i.e., towns with population over 1 million; percentage of total)	19,643 tpd (17.08%)
(c)	Waste generated in other Class 1 towns (towns with population over 0.1 million; percentage of total)	42,635 (37.07%)
(d)	Subtotal of (a), (b), (c) above (percentage of the whole)	83,378 (72.50%)

and above in a scientific manner, about 72.5 per cent, or roughly three-quarters of India's garbage can be effectively used.

The report also breaks down MSW (which varies from place to place depending on food habits) as follows:

The typical composition of MSW is as follows:

The collection and disposal of MSW is not very efficient in India. A study by the Central Pollution Control Board (CPCB) based on thirty-five cities states that the collection efficiency of MSW ranges between 22 and 60 per cent. It adds: 'About 40 per cent of all MSW is not collected at all and hence lies littered in cities/towns and finds its way to nearby drains and water bodies causing choking of drains and pollutions of surface water.'

• Compostable/biodegradable matter (can be converted into manure/fuel)	30% to 55%
• Inert material (to landfill)	40% to 45%
• Recyclable material	5% to 10%

Organic Wastes	51%
Recyclable	17%
Hazardous	11%
Inert	21%

It is often found that composting plants also do not function well in India; part of the reason may be that in urban areas it is difficult to market the compost which is needed more for agricultural fields. Residue-derived fuel (RDF) plants that produce electricity from garbage would make a significant difference. As early as the mid-1990s, the department of science and technology (DST) had fully demonstrated an RDF plant near Deonar, Mumbai, and subsequently built a plant at Hyderabad to use garbage to generate electricity; subsequent progress has to be accelerated.

Such garbage-to-electricity conversion plants are particularly useful not only because they generate much-needed electricity but also because they can use almost all waste material other than the inert materials. This means that the garbage landfill could be virtually eliminated: most of the waste material would be used to generate electricity, and the inert material could be used for road repair, and so on.

Once these technologies are perfected, much of the agricultural produce and biomass currently wasted in villages could also go to electricity-generating plants. What a boon this would be for rural India, since the agricultural waste would feed the grids and produce power for local consumption. As of now, much of the agricultural waste is just burnt as its disposal is costly.

There are other waste products to look at too, like building material wastes, waste from coal power stations, flyash, plastic waste, etc. Emphasis needs to be laid on these.

India has a good industry for converting scrap iron and steel received from many parts of the world into secondary steel. Some of these contain hazardous materials. Even while recovering the wastes, we should always ensure workers' safety and environmental safety. For example, electronics waste, which is going to be a huge area in the future, is often full of hazardous material. Even as we emphasize the importance of the 'Waste to Wealth' principle, enough attention needs to be given to make these operations safe.

Waste-water recovery and reuse should be taken up as a movement. The agriculture sector is the biggest user (80 per cent or more) of water, and this is where the biggest waste also occurs. But urban facilities like big apartment complexes, offices, hotels, etc., are equally culpable. Each of these should individually set up first-rate waste-water reuse facilities along with rainwater harvesting facilities. Educational institutions must also provide detailed courses on waste and water recovery and reuse, so that every citizen is made aware of what needs to be done.

Knowledge Chemistry

We would only like to point out one emerging field here which will become crucial for India in about a decade, by reducing waste at the process level itself. A whole set of such technologies are described in the TIFAC report on knowledge chemicals which we referred to in Chapter 8. This particular technology is known as process intensification (PI). To quote from the report:

> PI has the potential to increase the competitiveness of the chemicals industry by making processes faster, safer, high-yielding, energy-efficient and environment-friendly. According to the action plan for the implementation of process intensification prepared by Creative Energy of the Netherlands, implementation of PI has the potential of reducing around 20 per cent of the costs of the pharmaceutical industry in a span of 5–10 years and around 50 per cent in 10–15 years, through overall cost reduction from higher selectivity and process step integration.[2]

From Waste to Wealth

Another major area described in the TIFAC report is green manufacturing in which the pharmaceutical industry in Europe and the USA is making tremendous progress. This involves reducing solvent consumption, using better catalysts, using biocatalytic alternatives, using bio-renewable sources, etc. All these processes reduce costs because they nip in the bud various forms of wastage through the processes themselves.

What India Must Do to Prepare for the Future

In addition to stepping up waste recovery, waste reuse, waste minimization, etc., India needs to enter vigorously into the knowledge-intensive chemical processes too. These will be demanded in the future as the standards insisted on for chemical industries to follow. These in turn feed into virtually every industry.

The industries of the future will create wealth in the form of products made to desired standards and with little waste. They will be based on the principles of recycling and reuse.

Such is the world that we will see in a decade's time. India has to prepare for it now.

11 Health Care for All

Dr Kalam was born in 1931, sixteen years before Independence; Rajan was born in 1944. The life expectancy at that time was quite low: the national average was thirty-two years for a male and twenty-six years for a female. Today the average life expectancy of an Indian male is above sixty-seven years and that of an Indian female over sixty-nine years.[1] The life expectancy of an Indian woman is higher now than that of an Indian man—for the first time in history.

This is just a small example of the tremendous progress India has made in the health-care sector. Cholera and small pox, which claimed many Indian lives at the time of Independence, have been eradicated since. As we mentioned at the beginning of this book, polio has been eradicated too. Many other diseases like measles and whooping cough have disappeared. Malaria and tuberculosis are under control, as is HIV. The infant mortality rate in India has come down sharply and so has the mortality rate of women due to prenatal and postnatal infections.

Many of the above achievements are easily forgotten sometimes, because a lot more has to be done still in health care. But it is important to remember how these achievements took place. They were due to better availability of nutritious food and clean water, a general improvement in sanitation, a comprehensive vaccination programme, various targeted awareness programmes, better education (especially for women), and most importantly better access to doctors and health services, and the easy availability and inexpensive prices of essential medicines and life-saving drugs (thanks to our innovative and proactive pharmaceutical industry).

But still, ready access to medical services when one falls ill is a nightmare for many Indians. For the rich and powerful, of course, the whole world of modern health care is available. And for the few fortunate Indians who work in the organized sector (namely in the government, in public sector companies, and in medium and large private sector companies),[2] there is some form of health-care coverage. But most Indians are left high and dry. In theory, they can go to a nearby government hospital, stand in line, and avail of the relatively inexpensive medical consultation, testing and medication. In practice, however, government hospitals are far too few in number, and they lack management leadership. So most people depend on alternative medicine, like Ayurveda, Unani medicine, homeopathy, Siddha medicine, and so on. Only when an ailment is chronic or causing severe discomfort do they attempt to see an 'allopathic' doctor. Surveys indicate that even then about 80 per cent of such patients go to private doctors, nursing homes or small hospitals. Going to the big, branded private hospitals with the latest medical facilities is beyond the dreams of the average Indian.

The rough hierarchy of the government health delivery system, which caters to the majority of the population, is as follows:

- At the bottommost level are the Primary Health Centres (PHCs) or sub-PHCs. Operated by state governments, this is the first contact point for an Indian patient to approach a doctor for diagnostic and clinical advice. Not all PHCs are well equipped; often, there is a question mark over the regular attendance by doctors too. Even reasonably equipped PHCs suffer from India's great problem: the lack of regular electricity. Critical drugs that need refrigeration go bad as a result, and key equipment that needs electric power cannot be operated.

- The second level, where some hospitalization facilities are also available, is that of the secondary health care centres (SHCs). Normally located in the district headquarters—at a distance from the villages and nearby towns—these are, as can be expected, often overcrowded. They too suffer from an erratic electricity supply.

- Above these in the hierarchy are the large, well-equipped tertiary care hospitals which function in the state capitals or in a few other large cities. The tertiary care hospitals also run Emergency wards and Outdoor Patient Departments (OPDs).

- In addition to these, large public sector units have their own hospitals where they are located, for the benefit of their employees. The army has its own fully equipped medical set-up, and some Central government departments like DRDO, DAE and ISRO have moderate medical facilities for their employees as well. In addition to providing health insurance for their employees, some of the larger private sector companies have their own primary, secondary, and sometimes tertiary medical care systems as well.

Clearly, India has a long way to go before it can provide 'Health for All' as per the Alma-Ata declaration at the International Conference on Primary Health Care. Incidentally, this declaration, made in 1978, had a fulfilment target date of 2000.

The yawning gap that is left by government health-care services is filled in part by individual private practitioners and private hospital clinics. Not all of these are equipped with adequate pathological facilities or equipment. They have to make do with the limited experience and expertise they have. There are many private doctors operating all over India and many of them are unauthorized. But it should be realized that along with the cheap drugs provided by the pharmaceutical industry, these doctors are the mainstay of most patients. They are the doctors that most people who do not have the privilege of organized health-care services run to.

The real challenge before India is to provide the services of diagnostic laboratory tests, pathological and investigative tests, X-rays, ultrasounds, etc., at minimum cost to patients in all parts of the country. If these are readily available, private practitioners can use them as a starting point for treatment, with a lower likelihood of going completely wrong with the diagnosis.

Contradictory Demands

India's health-care needs vary from the very basic to the advanced. A large part of India's population leads a day-to-day existence, earning daily wages which too are often uncertain. People in this segment do not think of getting medical aid unless they are in a crisis situation. They are unable to pay even the very cheap costs for medical services in India. It is to the great credit of the implementers of the vaccination programmes that these programmes successfully reached all of these people, including their children.

But a better access to health care for every Indian citizen, beyond the vaccination programmes, would go a long way towards making life better for them and increasing their productivity, thus helping the economy as a whole. We have two suggestions that might help meet the high demand of medical care:

- Tele-education of the rural and small-town doctors to improve their clinical knowledge and update them on the latest developments in patient treatment.
- A large number of mobile diagnostic centres across the country, with modern equipment and a power generator, to reach people in remote corners.

While the connection of the poorer people to health care in India is rather tenuous, the demands of the middle class and the upper middle class from this sector are very high. They expect world-class facilities in the overworked, short-staffed government hospitals and small private hospitals. They want doctors to prescribe more diagnostic tests and the latest drugs, which are under patent protection and therefore very costly for the consumer. These demands not only put undue pressure on the health-care industry but also increase the disparities between the haves and the have-nots, which is not good for the country in the long run.

In the longer term, we might not have to worry about this at all. Once proper and comprehensive health insurance schemes are in place, people can demand the facilities and medications they want and pay for them through higher insurance premiums. But today most citizens draw health subsidies from the government kitty in one form or another, so the increased demands of the more well-to-do citizens puts additional pressure on the financial system, reducing the government's ability to provide somewhat better health care for the people who really need the government's help. Many states in the country have, however, introduced health-care systems and approved health-care centres for citizens below the poverty line (BPL).

In this context, it is interesting to note that a group of doctors at the All-India Institute of Medical Sciences (AIIMS) in Delhi, the leading medical institution in the country, have started an initiative called the Society for Less Investigative Medicine (SLIM). They point out that extensive medical research has established that most regular annual (or more frequent) check-ups for healthy persons are unnecessary and only add to health-care costs.[3]

Another area of concern is the growing prejudice against doctors and hospitals, when their decisions are constantly questioned and sometimes taken to court. We are certainly in favour of doctors and hospitals being accountable to the patients, and for bringing medical practice under the consumer protection law. But one must remember that for every wrong decision a doctor might make, he/she makes a hundred right ones, some of which actually save lives. The antagonistic mindset of patients only leads to doctors playing safe and prescribing more and more tests and consultations, adding needlessly to the cost of health care, which we must remember is mostly paid for from government funds.

Interestingly, the USA has the highest cost per person for health care in the world because of such litigations which are often encouraged by its own cartelized medical professionals. This is the reason why the richest country in the world is unable to reach easily accessible health care to the bottom 10–20 per cent of its citizens. If only it could reduce the oppressively severe system of medical litigations and place more trust in the doctors, the USA could have had a universal health-care system by now.

We must learn from the mistakes of the developed countries and evolve relatively inexpensive methods of health-care services that can reach every Indian.

Biomedical Equipment

An issue that is of great importance to health care in India is the local manufacture of biomedical equipment.

At the time of the IT boom in the 1990s, the government rightly gave a lot of incentives and tax concessions to the software industry; but it did not provide a similar support to the local manufacture of ICT hardware. This as we have seen has had a long-term detrimental effect on the economy. We depend far too much on imports, so much so that our current account deficit has now got out of hand. This is particularly a pity in a country like India which has a demographic advantage, where our human resources could be skilled to participate productively in local manufacturing and improve the economy.

It does not take much thought to realize that the use of biomedical equipment which is so crucial to health-care delivery and the prevention of diseases, is going to be a great drainer of foreign exchange for us, perhaps more than oil imports, unless we encourage local manufacturing.

Biomedical equipment is closely linked to electronics, advanced computational models and precision manufacturing technologies. These have developed to very high levels of sophistication over the past two decades. It is interesting to note that General Electric (GE), a global engineering giant, has set up an R&D centre for biomedical equipment in Bengaluru, to develop relatively inexpensive ultrasound equipment; the products from this facility are now sold in advanced countries like Japan. GE is not alone—there are about 400 such industrial R&D centres in India established by foreign multinational companies. This shows that the human resources and skills exist in India to adapt to the new demands. It is a challenge to our government and academic systems and industry that we are not channelizing these resources towards manufacturing competitive products locally.

It is essential that we step up local production of all biomedical equipment in India. An upsurge in local production will challenge many young Indian entrepreneurs to come up with new products of global standards as well, innovated and made in India for both Indian and global markets. The local manufacture of biomedical equipment is key, since this is the only way to keep the health-care system affordable and ensure that it can reach every Indian citizen, even those with very limited means.

Mobile Reach of Health Care

Before doctors and hospitals can treat patients, they must carry out diagnostics in the form of pathological tests. In today's India, the access to the equipment required for this is a problem. Huge investments in

PHCs are not cost effective; there are also problems with electricity and the availability of doctors.

TIFAC addressed this crucial problem as a follow-up to its Technology Vision 2020 exercise, of which the health-care sector was a major component. Based on several consultations, it came up with an idea which was at that time close to revolutionary: a mobile health-care facility that would reach everyone. A number of able doctors volunteered to work on the project in Uttarakhand on an experimental basis; the state government was also very cooperative.

The important elements of the project were:

- The doctors and important lab technicians and pharmacists would stay at Almora, a city with proper medical and communication facilities.
- A bus with diagnostic equipment would go on a specific route covering many villages. The time would be fixed with no changes allowed to the schedule. It would halt at places where there were no major SHCs. The villagers would come there.
- The main task of this Mobile Diagnostic Hospital and Research Centre would be to check the patient and give him/her test reports and medical advice. They would be charged nominally. Medicines would

be sold from the mobile unit for a few days; patients would buy subsequent doses from the market. For BPL persons as identified by the Uttarakhand government, medicines would be given free and diagnostic expenses would also be free for them.

• All the records would be computerized so that the loss of a medical history sheet would not affect patient care.

The challenge was to have all the lab equipment, ECG, X-ray and ultrasound unit, and an examination table fit into an ordinary bus, which is not longer than 24 ft. All the equipment ran on a 15 KVA noiseless diesel generator. It was a great system innovation which was achieved through excellent developmental engineering. Since TIFAC or the Uttarakhand government were not best equipped to run the operation regularly, a local partner, an engineering college at Bhimtal, was handed over the responsibility and paid for the services.

Conceived when Dr Kalam was still the chairman of the governing council of TIFAC and Y.S. Rajan the executive director, the project was a huge success. By the time it was formally launched in October 2002 by Dr Kalam, he had become the President of India. It was Y.S. Rajan's last major event at TIFAC—he would leave TIFAC the following month.

According to data from a research paper under preparation, the total number of camps organized in a period of about five and a half years (October 2002

TABLE 11.1   Statistics from Mobile Diagnostic Hospital and Research Centre, Uttarakhand (20 October 2002 to 31 March 2008)

1.	Total no. of districts covered by mobile hospital van	6
2.	Total no. of sites covered in one month	15
3.	Total no. of camps held	988
4.	Total no. of patients registered (a)	84449
5.	Total no. of revisits (b)	12029
6.	Total patient check-ups (a+b)	96478
7.	Total male patients' check-ups	28115
8.	Total female patients' check-ups	50845
9.	Total children patients' check-ups	5489
10.	Total BPL patients' check-ups	45644
11.	Total other patients' check-ups	38805
12.	Total no. of ultrasounds	20953
13.	Total no. of X-rays	9861
14.	Total no. of ECGs	2602
15.	Total no. of lab tests	38839
16.	Total distance covered by mobile van	92620 km

Source: Achla Khanna, TIFAC

to March 2008) was 1018 (almost one camp every alternate day, with only one scheduled camp that was missed in all this time). About 1 lakh patients were treated, of whom 54 per cent came under the BPL category and 60 per cent were women. It might be interesting to look at some more statistics from the report (Table 11.1).

Under the National Rural Health Mission (NRHM), 2005–12, this successful demonstration has resulted in the launch of 1951 Mobile Medical Units (MMUs) in 442 districts spread all over the country in PPP mode for the delivery of health-care services to difficult areas. In addition, 7097 Emergnecy Response Vehicles (ERVs) and 7458 ambulances for referral transport services have also been approved for implementation.

Such mobile health-care units need not be restricted only to difficult-to-access rural areas. They can make a real difference in providing health-care services to the poor and the lower middle class in towns and even cities. Our estimate is that every district should have at least three or four such mobile units; bigger towns can have more units, depending on population density. Overall, India can use at least 1000 more general-purpose Mobile Diagnostic Centres.

Health-Care Services as an Employment Generator

It is clear that health-care delivery is a human-intensive activity. Each patient needs individual care. There may be many machines to run diagnostics, but they still need to be operated. Human intervention is required at every step of the medical process. With health-care services aiming to reach every Indian, it is easy to see that the health-care sector can also be a major employment generator and strongly support the growing economy.

Dr Kalam explored these possibilities for the health-care sector in his address to the nation as President of India on Republic Day, 2005. We will end our discussion by quoting from his Action Plan for Employment Generation.

Another area which is an employment generator is the health-care industry. We have only one doctor for 1800 people, whereas in some of the developed countries the doctor to population ratio is 1:600. For providing quality health care to all of our citizens, we would need at least to double the strength of doctors and paramedical staff in the whole country. The investment for this need not necessarily come from the government alone. Hospitals can be set up by the private sector with certain tax concessions and subsidized infrastructural support.

Setting up of 30,000 static tele-medicine stations distributed in 30,000 key locations within the zone of 3 lakh villages and providing 20,000 mobile tele-medicines units will enable reaching of quality health care closer to every home, which are connected to the district, state government hospitals, corporate hospitals and super-speciality hospitals in the country. This is possible as India has a network of satellite communication.

How to reach health care to the large numbers of our population? An innovative method has come into action in certain states. This system provides free health cover to the citizens who are members and pay Rs 10 per individual per month as an insurance premium. The state and Central governments can sponsor this insurance scheme. Such an insurance cover should be able to provide for all types of diseases including expensive open heart surgery. A consortium is required to be formed in different states between the government, insurance agencies, corporate hospitals and NGOs for providing integrated, cost-effective health care. The scheme when fully operational can provide direct employment for an additional 600,000 doctors and 1.2 million paramedical staff. Apart from providing health care to citizens, these corporate hospitals can attract a large number of medical tourists to the country in view of our competitiveness in treating complex diseases.

CHAPTER

12 National Security
Strength, Intelligence
and Eternal Vigilance

The strategic sector is close to Dr Kalam's heart. His scientific career started with a defence laboratory; he then shifted to making rockets and satellite launch vehicles, which also happen to be the core elements of a missile, at ISRO; afterwards, he pioneered the first Indian missiles.

The strategic sector covers the military industries and also other core industries and technologies that support various other security functions of the nation such as intelligence gathering, vital communications required for military and internal security personnel, and so on. The sector now includes cyber security and our space assets as well.

In addition, there are many electronic and optoelectronic devices and special materials that find large-scale commercial applications that also form critical elements for national security-related equipment. For example, the optical sensors used for CCTVs in many shops and ATMs, in their advanced versions, become important for detecting border intrusions or keeping surveillance over vital installations. The same is true of many advanced microelectronic chips and nano systems with computing capabilities that are used in our PCs. These are termed dual-use technologies.

Many of these critical technologies were denied in the 1970s and 1980s, particularly to India's missile programme and space programme. With technological development in India, the access to these advanced technologies has now become easier.

Where Do We Stand?

In our book *India 2020* we had provided a road map for the strategic industries. The main thrust had been to move from the large import dependence to a predominant local dependence and then to predominant local production (even with foreign technologies or with foreign partnerships); the final step in this progression would be to move speedily to indigenous, India-designed, India-engineered and India-manufactured equipment, weapon systems, etc.

In 1998, when Dr Kalam was the scientific adviser to the defence minister, the minister had convened a meeting of industry leaders, defence services, defence production agencies, DRDO and others, to evolve an urgent action plan for the indigenization of production and the induction of R&D into industries for future systems. The reports were convincing and there was a consensus on the action plan from all the stakeholders. A target of changing the import-to-local-production ratio from 70:30 in 1998 to 30:70 in ten years' time was set and a committee headed by Dr Kalam was formed to evolve a ten-year profile leading to a 70 per cent indigenous defence system.

In the following decade, apart from our missile programme, strategic missiles got into production and deployment. A successful programme has been that of the BrahMos missile, designed and produced as a joint venture between Russia and India, and named after the Brahmaputra and Moscova rivers. Its success has been phenomenal and it has met the user trials of all the three services, the army, navy and air force, and was inducted by them into operational service. The BrahMos missile is a great demonstration of the fact that India can produce world-class defence equipment.

But, reviewing the situation as of 2014, we have still not reached the target of a 70 per cent indigenous defence system as had been visualized. India has in fact become the largest importer of defence equipment and systems in the world—a top spot not to be very proud of. Such huge imports of defence equipment is not good for our overall national security. In addition, such an import dependence causes a very heavy drain of foreign exchange, leading to a larger current account deficit. And, above all, by not having much local production in defence equipment, we lose millions of jobs for Indians every year.

What we need is a revolution for self-sufficiency in defence equipment and systems, and evolving a defence industrial complex including private and government sectors, much like the Green Revolution in agriculture. In this chapter we will look at how we can achieve this revolution. Drawing upon India's rich traditions, we have named our action plan the Drona Revolution.

India's Security Situation

India's security situation today is much more complex than what it was during the 1990s. The low-intensity terrorist attacks did pose a serious threat, but their impact was not felt by the people in general. The nuclear explosions conducted by India in 1998 changed the strategic equations. Many sanctions were imposed against India by the international community; but these were relaxed quite soon since the huge Indian market could not be ignored for long by the leading companies in the developed countries, and also since India had started building a high-technology capacity.

However, the economic growth path in post-liberalization India took the safer route of depending upon the services sector and relying on the import route. The balanced approach of building technology strengths within Indian industries, as recommended in the Vision 2020 exercises, was ignored by the policymakers, administrators and industry leaders alike. Technology development and engineering innovations took a back seat.

A similar easy approach was taken in terms of not taking decisive action against terrorism exported into the country from beyond our borders. Terrorist modules began to build up within India. Very little was done in terms of using modern technologies and organizational systems to track down terrorists and punish them. When we see how difficult the USA made it for terrorists to operate in their country after the 9/11 attacks, we can see how lax India's approach was in comparison.

Little is known about our plans to equip the police and paramilitary forces to track terrorist movement. We do have a basic intelligence infrastructure, but much of it needs to be upgraded to keep up with the use of modern technologies by the terrorists. New areas of concern to the national security such as cyber security need immediate attention. To compound the problem, in recent years some critical defence purchases have been on hold due to allegations of scams.

It is necessary for all Indians to realize that a lot more needs to be done in the area of national security, viz.

- modernizing our defence forces rapidly to make up for lost time,
- indigenization of defence production,
- strengthening and skilling internal security systems against various forms of terrorism, and
- preparing India to be cyber secure.

If citizens really demand 'zero tolerance' against terrorism and are prepared to make some key changes in our public life to meet such a demand, then India can be secure. As India grows economically, socially and in knowledge, enemy attacks in various forms will only increase. It is imperative that we build a culture to maintain 'eternal vigilance', on all fronts.

The Drona Action Plan

The first and foremost task is to achieve a high degree of production of defence and internal security equipment in India. From the experience of the past six decades, it is easy to see that such a task cannot be accomplished by the public sector units and ordinance factories alone; the door has to be kept open for the private sector and foreign companies. There are serious debates now, as in the past, as to how much FDI should be allowed in the defence sector. Defence technologies are very sophisticated and complex; foreign defence businesses can be expected to manufacture equipment and systems in India only when they have full control over their business. On the other hand, there are no major technological strengths for defence production in most Indian companies. Our approach therefore should be, for the next decade at least, to aim for large-scale manufacture of defence equipment and systems in India without placing unnecessary restrictions on the foreign companies or Indian private companies that come forward.

Naturally, these companies cannot thrust their products on the defence and internal security services. They will have to work with the defence and security services to take care of their customer needs just as they do in any other business. At the same time, the political leadership should clearly tell the defence and security services that they should avoid imports as much as possible and procure primarily from units manufacturing in India. A broad guideline for the percentage of indigenous procurement should be given and monitored.

Foreign and Indian companies should be given the freedom to decide their manufacturing plan. They may not be able to manufacture all items in India; they may need to procure some critical components and assemblies from abroad. Still, one should not resort to the methods of the earlier era of the Phased Manufacturing Programme (PMP) which failed to indigenize quality production. A full-scale manufacturing unit with knock-down and semi-knock-down imports of all assemblies, simply integrating these as kits in India, should not be allowed; this would defeat the purpose of developing local manufacturing.

Since the companies have to compete to meet customer needs and take risks to diversify their markets, they should be allowed full freedom to export as well. If needed, a small export denial list can be given for select items; most foreign companies will already have such a list from the countries of their origin in Europe or the USA.

The goal is to start a major defence industry in India operated by Indian and foreign companies. Once this is set up, it will have a tremendous impact on Indian industry. Our engineering colleges will also start orienting themselves to supply suitably skilled human resources.

This Big-Bang start should be the first important and essential step of the Drona Revolution. The target should be to have 80 per cent local production and 20 per cent imports for all our defence and security equipment near the year 2025, a decade from now.

The second step of the Drona Action Plan would be to identify the critical elements for local production. The starting point should be to have Indian design and development facilities for a few critical items, with full respect for the IPRs of other countries. This activity should not be left to a national laboratory or academic institutions, but should be done by a consortium of industries and R&D laboratories. They may be able to sell their inventions to the production companies operating in India or abroad. The products will also form a reserve backup in case technology is denied to India by foreign powers at a later point in time.

The third, and parallel, step would be to continually better the existing systems through small, incremental improvements in order to meet the new needs of defence and internal security services. These incremental improvements, which may take place in the hundreds, will make India's defence and internal security systems much more agile, alert and advanced. This effort should be led by industries in close association with the actual customers, namely the defence services, intelligence services and internal security services.

The fourth step would be to decide upon and define the details of an India-specific security system with a geopolitical view, just as China has done for its protection from the Pacific Ocean–based attacks. For India some key areas to look at might be land border protection from infiltration, protection of the eastern coast, action against pirate activity in the Arabian Sea to protect Indian ships entering the Gulf region, a vigil kept on the Indian Ocean, and so on. The decision on the priority areas may be determined by the political leadership and the defence and security services. DRDO and other scientific organizations may need to take the lead in this, in close association with the operational services and other stakeholders.

The fifth step would be to work on an innovative India-conceived and India-designed system for defence and the internal security service. This does not need to be a mega system; perhaps one sub-system added to the existing system can be a game changer. The lead for this must come from the national laboratories and the Indian industry's R&D wing. These innovations need to be closely guarded and their IPRs vigilantly protected.

If all five 'fingers' of the Drona Action Plan are initiated simultaneously and sincerely, we can easily achieve the Drona Revolution in a decade, near the year 2025. This action plan can completely transform India and establish it as a world leader on the global stage. As Dr Kalam is fond of saying, 'Strength respects strength.'

Comprehensive National Security

This is not enough, however. Another area in which we have to move very fast is that of cyber security, with all its dimensions of protection, security and offensive attacks. Our vigilance on this front cannot be confined to defence, internal security and governance systems alone. Cyber security is needed by all citizens—it applies to a railway booking system, a net banking operation, a mass entertainment system, a social media profile, and hundreds of other things that an ordinary citizen engages with on a regular basis. We need to devise an action plan that can guarantee the cyber safety of each individual citizen.

India has taken small steps in cyber safety, which are simply not enough. The field of cyber security is changing so fast that it requires the agility of a sprinter and the tenacity of marathon runner on the part of the government to keep up. This is an area where we must sprint the marathon.

For every Indian to feel safe and enjoy the fruits of development, the Drona Revolution and a high-speed action plan for cyber security are critical.

We will end this chapter with a brief quote from the presidential address to the nation by Dr Kalam delivered on 14 August 2006, the eve of India's sixtieth Independence Day. This outlines how each one of us can make a positive difference to national security.

Peaceful and harmonious conditions in all parts of the country are essential for people to cooperate with one another for accelerated national growth.

However, there are challenges to peace from across our geographical borders, from terrorism and violence, and from scarcities created by rapidly depleting natural resources. These dynamic challenges call for special measures to ensure a comprehensive, integrated system of security which has four major components: territorial security, internal security, energy security and economic security.

Internal security is an important aspect of security that is drawing the attention of the entire country and the world. The constant threat of low-intensity proxy war and terrorism has become a disturbing feature of national life. This constitutes the new face of war. This matter is of great concern to all of us. Therefore I propose to share my thoughts with you on how we can face this challenge and resolve to eradicate that threat.

At the state level, greater and more effective coordinated decision-making ability is the most basic requirement. At individual levels, greater respect for traditional values and a sense of social responsibility like love and respect for one's family and teachers, service to the neighbourhood and community, tolerance for authority are now absolutely essential. Above all, we as people, individuals and especially institutions require an increased ability to cooperate with one another, improving thereby our work and personal relationships. While we have the basic structure in the form of law, police cadres, intelligence agencies and the judicial system, we need to reinforce them with required updates with a code of conduct. Every citizen, every group, every religion and every political and executive system should allow the law to function without interference.

National Security

with one world in improving the lives and prospects . . . have taken some steps in this direction . . . agencies in the field . . . equipped to furnish them with . . . required up to date . . . trouble. Every citizen, every group, every religion and every national and executive system that follow the law to the goal without interference.

CHAPTER 13 Education for Every Indian

Education is the most important element for the growth and prosperity of a nation. India is in the process of transforming itself into a developed nation. Yet we have 350 million people who are not literate and many more who need to acquire employable skills to fit into the emerging modern India and current global trends.

Children who belong to the weaker sections of our society are undernourished, and only a small percentage of them manage to complete eight years of satisfactory education. We need to think specifically about them. Education is a fundamental right of every Indian child. Can we allow a situation to continue in which millions of children are forced into lifelong poverty? The requirement is that parents should be able to go to any nearby school, admit their children there and return home with the confidence that their children will get a good and value-based quality education. Differently abled children require equally focused attention. In view of such critical issues, and also to break out of our historical mindset, an effective and self-renewing education system is the need of the hour in India. Such a system is in fact fundamental to the survival and growth of civilizations.

We now propose to address the issues pertaining to education in some detail and suggest some solutions that can be considered for implementation.

Inequality of Access to Educational Resources

Unequal access to educational resources still exists due to a variety of reasons. For example, we have seen three types of families in our villages. The fortunate ones are those who realize the importance of educating their children at any cost and guide them at all critical stages; they are able to do so due to their economic well-being. Then there are those families who might realize the importance of education, but are not aware of the opportunities nor of the procedures and ways to realize these opportunities for their children. There is a third category of families that are economically weak and also do not realize the value of education; hence for generations together their children are neglected and continue to live in poverty.

It is essential that we enlighten and create a widespread awareness of education among all sections of society, particularly in rural areas and among the urban poor. We should use technology for this important social purpose. It is possible for NGOs, other social and philanthropic institutions and the media to focus on this area of creating awareness. We should also mobilize necessary resources for providing education to underprivileged people. Let us elaborate the way ahead.

The Mission of Education

Over the last sixty-seven years, successive governments have been committed to achieve the national goal of universal education and have steadily increased the budgetary allocation for education. However, 35 per cent of our adult population is yet to achieve literacy. The expenditure on education as a percentage of our GDP has a direct impact on our literacy. Today our expenditure on education in India is little more than 4 per cent of our GDP. If we have to achieve nearly

100 per cent literacy, it is necessary to increase the expenditure on education to about 6 to 7 per cent of GDP. This 2 to 3 per cent increase has to be sustained only for a few years. Thereafter, a lower percentage of GDP allocation to education will be adequate to sustain the high degree of literacy in this country.

Clearly, public expenditure alone from governments at the Centre and in the states might not able to meet the challenge of mobilizing an additional 2 to 3 per cent of GDP for the mission of education. It is here that we have to generate additional resources for this noble mission. Expenditure on education, whether at the Centre or in the states, can no longer be provided only by the respective ministries or departments for human resource development. Indeed, every department must play a significant role as a partner of the human resource development organization, and contribute resources in terms of budget and infrastructure for implementing the mission of providing quality education to the whole nation.

To augment the government resources, the entire corporate sector has to emulate the example set by some corporate leaders who have focused on education to make a national difference. Different regions of the country may be adopted by the corporate sectors within an overall national mission for education. The mechanism should enable the corporates to have freedom to innovate and deliver directly.

Planning for Good Education

The preferred school concept that we have today has come about as a result of differential quality and standards of teaching. There is a need to make the quality of teaching high in all schools. There is also a need for preparatory education—even in rural areas— to make the child competitive when he or she joins the regular school. For running such schools in rural areas, NGOs and the corporate sector can play a vital role. Moreover, rich parents who can afford the expense can sponsor the preparatory school education for a certain number of rural children.

When Dr Kalam visited Etawah in Uttar Pradesh as President of India, Master Kuldeep Yadav, a student of class ten, asked him the following question:

> Villages are also full of talent but facilities are available only in the towns/cities. Have you planned something for these children so that they can get good education in the villages?

We need to address this problem, which has multiple dimensions. There is the non-availability of infrastructural facilities in schools, the problem of syllabi followed in the school and the non-availability of quality teachers.

Job opportunities being national in scope, the syllabus should be structured in such a manner that it meets the changing societal needs, fulfils the needs of emerging occupations, and inculcates high moral values among the students in addition to learning skills. The delivery of quality education is possible only through quality teachers. The teacher has to be committed, must love teaching and children, and must be equipped with all the knowledge required for effective teaching. The self-esteem of the teacher must be high and he/she must have the quality to become a role model for the children. Some element of competitive rewarding based on performance should be there. This competency has to be built up throughout the country through a massive teachers' education programme delivered through a continuously updated tele-education system. This can be funded and implemented by a consortium of government and educational institutions with the corporate sectors providing value-added services.

There is an urgent need that every school should have basic amenities such as a good building equipped with ventilated, well-lit, airy and spacious classrooms besides a good library, laboratories including the latest IT tools and infrastructure, safe drinking water, clean toilets and a playground. This is all possible by earmarking the additional 2 to 3 per cent of GDP to education.

Keeping Children in School

It is reported that 39 per cent of children drop out of school after studying till class five and 55 per cent drop out after studying up to class eight. This situation needs remedial action, especially since assent has been accorded for the 86th Constitution Amendment Act: the Right to Education Bill for children between the ages of five and fourteen. But an act alone cannot achieve the goal unless education is delivered in a manner which will take into account the socio-economic reality and perception of the people to whom it is addressed. Apart from attracting children to schools, the education system should be able to provide nourishment and inject creativity among the children. The aim of the education system should also be to build character and human values, enhance learning capacity through technology and build confidence among children to face the future.

An education model implemented in Karnataka provides accelerated learning using computer aids so that children can have a creative learning experience with the tools of innovative animation through computers. This holistic phenomenon of learning, once ingrained in the primary stage where there is a happy learning process and non-threatening evaluation, will lead to voluntary learning by the participants.

Examination Reforms

Many children and their parents complain about too many entrance examinations which the children have to appear in for entry into schools, colleges, universities and professional courses. This is indeed a heavy burden on our young citizens. Also, it has led to a proliferation of tuitions and coaching institutes for preparing the students for entrance examinations.

For entry into universities and professional colleges, we have to devise a common all-India examination to be conducted by a nominated institution of the government. The examination must be so designed that attending a coaching course does not provide undue advantage to privileged students. The entrance test should be more in the nature of aptitude assessment.

There is a demand for a more transparent and reliable system of examination, evaluation and reporting. It has been noticed that today's examinations primarily test the memory of the students. In the 1950s, we used to have open-book examinations, which actually made it a tough examination for the students. We would recommend that the examining bodies may consider the introduction of an open-book system of examination. This will promote creativity among the teachers in setting questions and make for an evaluation of the creative ability of the students. A secure examination system is the need of the hour.

The examining bodies should have a reliable evaluation system and timely declaration of results. Special training must be carried out by the examining bodies to certify the examiners in the evaluation process. The examining bodies must evolve very good procedures and get quality certifications for their evaluation system.

Technology-Enhanced Education

Constraints of time and space together with the rapid obsolescence of knowledge in some areas of science and technology have created a huge demand for different courses from different institutions in the distance mode. There is a need for a working digital library system that alone can, in the long run, provide the kind of access required for a knowledge society. Technology-enhanced learning is a solution. It attempts to exploit the rapid developments in information and communication technology. As the communications bandwidth continues to increase and the cost of computer power continues to drop, technology-enhanced learning will become an economically viable solution. Virtual classrooms of the future will have students from many locations taught by a team of geographically distributed instructors through tele-education delivery systems.

Employment Generation

Our employment generation system has not kept up pace with the inflow of educated youth. A three-pronged strategy is needed to make education more attractive and simultaneously create employment potential.

Firstly, the educational system should highlight the importance of entrepreneurship and prepare the students right from the college stage to get oriented towards setting up enterprises. Diversity of skills and perseverance in work makes an entrepreneur. In addition, college syllabi, even for arts, science and commerce courses, should include topics and practicals where such entrepreneurship is possible.

Secondly, the banking system should provide venture capital right from the village level to prospective entrepreneurs for undertaking new enterprises. Banks have to be proactive in supporting innovative products for enabling wealth generation by young entrepreneurs by setting aside the conventional 'tangible asset' syndrome.

Thirdly, there has to be an economic pull for the generation of marketable products and enhancement of purchasing power among the people. This can come through implementation of mega programmes such as rural connectivity, regional linking of rivers, infrastructural missions, power missions and tourism.

We need our education system to focus on and be oriented towards high value and productive employment opportunities. A recent study indicates that the unemployment level in the country is 9 per cent; with 400 million employable people in India, the number of unemployed is around 36 million. We can definitely find productive employment for all these 36 million people by launching certain missions like bio-diesel generation through plants such as jatropha, and dry land and herbal farming in the available 33 million ha of wasteland earmarked for cultivation.

In his foreword to Y.S. Rajan's book *Way Beyond the Three Rs*, Dr Kalam summarizes the employment mission with respect to education:

During their graduation years students should be taught economically and socially relevant specializations. Similarly during the secondary school stage, students should be made proficient in relevant skills.

By the time their education is over, students should have the belief that they can fit into the employment market. In some cases, they even become employment generators instead of employment seekers.[1]

Conclusion

Ultimately, education in its real sense is the pursuit of truth. It is an endless journey through knowledge and enlightenment. Such a journey opens up new vistas of development of humanism where there is no scope nor room for pettiness, disharmony, jealousy, hatred or enmity. It transforms a human into a wholesome being, a noble soul and an asset to the universe. Universal brotherhood in its true sense forms the core of such education. Real education enhances the dignity of a human being and increases his or her self-respect. If only the real sense of education could be realized by each individual, and carried forward in every field of human activity, the world would be a much better place to live in.

To quote Dr Kalam again from the foreword to *Way Beyond the Three Rs*, the point of a good education system should be that:

People with a much higher ability of thinking and taking action should be given enough opportunities to take creative risks. What they need is more freedom and a system that supports bold ideas and does not punish them.

The mission of education in India is to provide a foundation to ensure the creation of enlightened citizens who will make India a prosperous, happy and strong nation in the future.

14 Emerging Technologies
Catching Up and Forging Forward

In the previous chapters we have discussed where India stands in the world today with respect to various sectors like agriculture, manufacturing, education and health care, and where we are in terms of meeting domestic needs and demands. We have also looked at the opportunities we have missed and the problems still facing us. The reason for this exercise has been to ensure that we do not repeat our past mistakes as we forge our way forward.

As a nation we tend to become complacent too soon when we see some early success, and forget that there is an immense amount of hard work to be done before we can achieve our goals. As we rest on our scant laurels and pat ourselves on the back, many an opportunity to better ourselves passes by. If we had not let go of half the opportunities we have missed since the 1970s, India would by now have forgotten what poverty is. We should learn from the example of South Korea, which in 1970 was in a condition much worse than what India was like then, and look at the progress it has made by leaps and bounds since.

It was the economic liberalization in 1991 that jolted India into action. The Technology Vision 2020 exercises, undertaken soon after, charted an ambitious way forward for growth and development. Had the approach, directions and road map outlined in the Vision 2020 exercises been followed closely by the government and industries, today, in 2014, we would no longer have been talking about 'catching up' with the rest of the world. Over the past two decades, we would have caught up and would be charting the way forward, as China has done. We would have been concentrating today on the last lap in the project of making India a developed country by the year 2020, completing the processes started much earlier. There would have been thousands of innovative start-ups in India and the knowledge–skill ecosystem that would have evolved would have led to the nations of the world making India their base. Venture capitalists from around the world would be hovering around India, and our economy would have been strong.

All this sounds like a dream now. India did not follow the relatively tough path suggested by the Vision 2020 exercises to achieve a sustainable 10 per cent GDP growth rate continuously for ten years.

However, India has made rapid progress in many sectors even amidst fluctuating GDP growth rates since 1991.

Let us explore the achievements of India. The developed-India Vision 2020 has been progressing slowly under successive governments. Today, India has made substantial progress in enhancing agricultural productivity, increasing per capita income and extending IT and IT-enabled services exports to over $86 billion. The pharma industry has grown to a $15 billion business; the Indian automobile industry has become the third largest in the world with 2.8 million vehicles produced in 2014; India has become the world's second largest mobile-phone user with 900 million users; we have explored the moon with *Chandrayaan-1* and found water there. In addition, large-scale infrastructure has been created as a part of rural and urban development missions such as multi-lane roadways and modern airport infrastructure; all-weather rural roads are being developed. The current literacy rate in India stands at 74.04 per cent (in 2012). India's health-care sector is projected to grow to nearly $40 billion and a quality health-care infrastructure will reach eighteen states by 2015. We are aspiring to provide clean green energy and safe drinking water to all the citizens of the nation.

With this growth, we have to assess where we are in terms of what we aspired to in the 1990s, and where the gap in achievement might be. It is time for us to take up a review mission to inspect the gap and suggest methods by which we can accelerate progress, so that by 2020 and beyond, India can become a developed country with zero poverty, 100 per cent literacy, quality health care for all, a value system—embedded quality education for all, and value-added employment for every citizen consistent with his/her education and professional skills.

This has to be done as a techno-economic programme with clear directions to the Central and state governments and an empowered, efficient and accelerated administrative governance system. The review should enable economists to work out the rise of GDP growth from the existing 4.5 per cent and scientists and technologists to determine the method by which they can achieve the desired growth and sustain that growth till the year 2020 and beyond.

The policies that are needed to realize sustainable economic development include:

- Enacting sustainable and inclusive economic policies
- Shedding the old, archaic laws, rules, regulations and procedures that are stumbling blocks and extractive in nature
- Creating a single-window facilitation centre fixing the responsibilities and QoS (Quality of Service) parameters for clearing projects
- Removing abrasive tax structures to allow the industry and service sector to thrive and encourage the people to save
- Restructuring and resizing the ministries and implementing a secured, dynamic workflow–based e-governance system to provide accelerated and efficient governance
- Establishing agro-food processing to market ecosystem with value addition to farm produce
- Creating an Indian industrial investment ecosystem to empower small and medium enterprises and skill development to provide more employment

generation in agro-food processing, industry and service sectors

- Creating an enabling environment for establishing modular solar farms and seawater desalination plants
- Announcing the immediate implementation of an ethanol policy to promote sugar cultivation and reduce oil imports
- Activating tourism, hospitality and rural sector development with corporate tax exemption and creating more employment opportunities with achievable targets, among others.

In order to realize this growth rate sustainably for the next ten years, we should explore our strengths, our core competencies and the expected levels of creative leadership to be provided over the next decade. Our principal core competence is agriculture. We therefore need to start with agriculture and the related sectors to create a sustainable economic infrastructure.

India has already achieved food security by producing 265 million tonnes of food a year. According to a World Economic Forum report, over the past few years, food insecurity and the global economic crisis have highlighted the urgent need for developing sustainable agricultural systems. Nearly 1 billion people—one out of six globally—lack access to adequate food and nutrition. By 2050, the global population will surpass 9 billion and the demand for agricultural products will double. Economically speaking, the agro-food sector is more promising than any other, given its size, its global reach and the fact that food security is a basic need for all of us. With its track record in agriculture, India should now launch a second revolution mission to achieve 350 million tonnes of food production a year by around 2020. We should launch an integrated agriculture and food processing mission coupled with agriculture-related manufacturing, industry and service sector missions. Our ultimate aim should be to capture at least 40 per cent of the global agri-food market by 2050. This would require an annual investment of around $50 billion and would entail the development of several related areas. In order to realize this mission, we have to create an enabling economic infrastructure.

The indicators of sustainable development are the per capita consumption of energy, water, coal and steel. The consumption of these ingredients is directly proportional to the developmental status of any nation. Our economic policies should help increase our use of these elements to the world average and above, so as to bring about development.

- *Steel*: We need to convert iron ore into finished steel and reduce our imports, in the process increasing our per capita steel consumption by ten times, that is, to 670 million tonnes by 2020.
- *Coal*: India ranks twenty-fifth in the world in per capita consumption of coal while China ranks first. We need to increase our coal production and consumption by seven times to 2000 million tonnes by 2020 by removing legal bottlenecks through parliamentary laws and by following transparent and proactive policies to make efficient use of our natural resources.
- *Energy*: Our mission should be to achieve energy independence by 2030, to free the nation from fossil-fuel dependence. India's per capita power consumption was 684 KWH as of 2011; we ought to increase it by at least five times by 2020. Creation of a high-voltage power grid to productively use the power being generated and reduce transmission and distribution losses is absolutely essential.
- *Water*: In India, the per capita consumption of water is 135 litres per person per day. The per capita water availability is reducing progressively and has reduced to 1545 cubic metres as per the 2011 census. This will reduce sharply to 1340 cubic metres by 2025

and further to 950 cubic metres by 2050. India has to plan to improve its storage capacity which currently is a mere 200 cubic metres per capita. The challenge is to identify the water management systems and practices that will increase availability. The target for per capita water availability should be 2500 cubic metres by 2025, rising further to 5000 cubic metres by 2050. For this to happen, we need to launch a smart waterways grid mission to harness the 1500 billion cubic metres of flood water and channelize this into our 15,000 km–long waterways, which will feed all the bigger dams more than twice a year.

With these achievements and proposed sustainable economic development plan and polices, let us look at the more exciting area of mastering emerging technologies, so that beyond 2025, we do not just play catch-up any longer but also make our presence felt as a world leader.

Agriculture

These are the major tasks required in the agriculture sector to catch up with the best in the world and realize our own full potential.

1. *Increase productivity of all arable lands* through the use of modern agronomic practices. A good place to start is by testing the soil in order to match the fertilizer and micronutrient inputs to the type of crops to be grown. This method has successfully transformed agriculturists' lives in Bihar through Vision 2020 projects. The National Agro Foundation (NAF), set up by the late C. Subramaniam, tests soils and gives agronomic advice to farmers in Tamil Nadu. India requires a hundred such foundations to transform agriculture technologically.

2. *Monsoon-proof agriculture.* This has to be done through a variety of forms focusing on the availability of water from the seeding stage to the seedling stage and later. The goal is to protect the plants throughout from water stress. Micro-irrigation, drip irrigation, lake irrigation, and so on, are some methods that can be used for this. In many places used-water recycling and reuse, along with rainwater harvesting, would help. In some places selective use of ground water may also be needed. Satellite remote sensing methods along with GIS (geographic information system) can help in the periodic monitoring of the soil-moisture status all over India.

3. *Increase production per hectare* to almost double the present capacity in most parts of India. If (1) and (2) above are achieved, with the right rotation of crops, it is possible to have two or even three croppings a year in most arable lands. At this point GM crops may also be introduced speedily. Indian agriculture production will leap forward if this is done.

4. *Provide export and marketing freedom for agri-products.* The increased production will directly benefit the consumers and farmers, but only when the current restrictions on the freedom to market are removed. We also need to aggressively export; this will require special help from the government and corporate sector to the farmers.

5. *Provide improved animal health care.* As a part of the agriculture sector, an area requiring immediate attention is veterinary care. Though India has a very large network of veterinary centres, their services are quite poor. It is worthwhile handing over many of these centres to active organizations like the Bharatiya Agro Industries Foundation (BAIF). Some animal health-care work could also be privatized. Similarly, fisheries and poultry farms need to expand to meet the growing domestic needs and to capture export markets.

6. *Improve agricultural infrastructure.* All the items above require various forms of infrastructure—roads from and to the fields, storage facilities, air-conditioned storage for some items, transport facilities, and the like, electricity of course and, going forward, broadband connectivity. The government has to take the lead in providing these facilities without imposing restrictive conditions on the users. Some of the work could also be done by the private sector or even foreign investors.

7. *Promote agro-food processing and agri-waste processing industries* in villages and nearby small towns. These are crucial for agricultural reforms because a large number of persons who are financially dependent on agriculture need to be weaned away from their land dependence to higher-paying jobs in agriculture infrastructure, agro-industries, retail, transport, storage, tourism and construction sectors where they can easily adapt.

8. When all the seven steps above take root and people start seeing the change, launch the major agriculture reform movement of consolidating the fragmented lands to be run by corporatized cooperatives or private sector cooperatives. This process can launch India into the next phase of high-growth

and globally competitive agriculture. This will lead to prosperity in agriculture and many young entrepreneurs will be attracted to the agriculture sector (including animal husbandry and forestry) as a profession. They will be 'agropreneuers', earning as much as entrepreneurs in other sectors.

Manufacturing

Agriculture can be liberated only if a large number of persons who are dependent on agriculture can be absorbed into the manufacturing sector. The Indian manufacturing sector faces a threefold challenge before it can catch up with the world and meet all domestic needs.

1. *Build low-end, relatively simple-skilled MSMEs* to absorb huge populations from rural and urban areas into productive activities, to meet domestic and export demands.
2. *Catch up in medium- and high-tech areas of manufacturing* (from materials, machines and capital goods to electronics and optoelectronics). The manufacturing sector in India has suffered about a quarter century of neglect, especially post-liberalization. In many

areas of electronics, telecom, and the like, India has been 'deindustrialized'. We need to catch up on a few decades of negligence.

3. *Go beyond (1) and (2) into many emerging areas of manufacturing.* In these areas, countries like China and Malaysia have progressed a great deal and India has a lot of catching up to do. These areas require high knowledge intensity and much greater integration of computing and automation systems, in addition to the use of advanced materials. Such areas are not just in electronics or aeronautics but also in sectors of power generation, mining, textiles, biomedicals, etc.

We have addressed many of these areas in detail earlier. Here we would like to emphasize the important catch-up areas for manufacturing.

(a) The electronics sector has had a history of missed opportunities ever since the 1970s. Homi Bhabha and Vikram Sarabhai's vision, identifying it as a crucial sector for the future, led to a special department in the Central government. Unfortunately, instead of promoting the industry, the department became a dreaded controller of emerging industries. The result is that India has missed about forty years of cumulative experience in the field, so much so that in the Indian launch vehicles or missiles, while almost all elements are indigenized, we are still dependent on many electronics components from abroad. Our telecom sector is entirely import-dependent, as is the computer sector, fibre optics and biomedical equipment.

To catch up without foreign players is difficult and may take years. India should give special incentive packages to those who invest in India to create greenfield projects for all electronic and optoelectronic items—devices to assemblies to systems. India should specially incentivize the establishment of R&D centres in India by foreign MNCs in electronic products, devices, materials, and so on. These could be manufactured in special electronics export zones (SEEZs). FDI in defence may also give special consideration to electronics industries, as defence electronics will boost high-tech electronics industries in India.

(b) In traditional sectors like textiles, leather, agro-food processing, and so on, there is a need to target the manufacturing of machines in India. To start with, these may contain many imported assemblies but over the period of a decade most of them should be sourced in India.

(c) In the area of heavy machinery, capital goods, and so on, India has lost its edge. Most of the machines used in building highways or high-rise buildings in India are imported; we see an Indian company's name as a marketer or assembler at best. The machine tool sector is 80 per cent import-dependent. Even many agricultural machineries need updates in technology. Using various incentives, many foreign machine manufacturing companies should be attracted to come to India and start greenfield plants or have joint ventures with Indian companies. India's tag of being 'the most difficult country to do business with' needs to be removed in order to attract them.

(d) As part of the catch-up process, India should aim to have about ten mega manufacturing industries on a global scale operating within the borders of India by 2020. These industries need not all be owned by Indians; they may have a foreign ownership or be joint ventures. The huge Indian workforce working for such companies will be a great asset for India in the years beyond 2020.

Natural Resources

Swami Vivekananda chastised Indians not to be just 'hewers of wood and drawers of water'. He emphasized the need for them to go up in the value chain. India is blessed with many mineral resources, but sadly we have just been extractors of ores and exporters of raw ores. We import both coal and iron ore for our domestic needs.

We need to revive our mining industry with utmost speed. This will also be a great job creator for the Indian workforce. We need to:

(a) adopt safe mining practices,

(b) increase value addition within India, preferably near the mines as it will also provide higher-income jobs for the locals,

(c) let the public sector mining companies be restructured or even privatized, and

(d) enable foreign investors to come to India with a focus on more value addition in India.

In addition to speedily executing the above, we must also carry out extensive surveys to find more mineral resources. Many experts are of the opinion that India has not explored and surveyed its mineral wealth potential fully. Among the elements that should be particularly focused on for exploration are rare earths and uranium sources.

Infrastructure

This is an area where there is an all-round slowness in implementation. We must:

(a) Speed up existing approved projects.
(b) Take forward projects in the pipeline by clearing all hurdles and finding pragmatic solutions to environmental issues. There could be a special empowered mechanism to take care of legitimate grievances of displaced persons, and also to clear the backlog of earlier promises made by governments.

Roads are of crucial importance, as is the availability of 24×7 electricity. Railways and inland and coastal waterways are helpful additions to infrastructure. We should start as many smart waterways as possible at the state level, and finally create a national smart waterways grid. We should also revive many of the old small airports built during the Second World War; this would connect many Tier I towns with air access.

While doing the above, we must also bear in mind that we need to help the Indian manufacturing sector by incentivizing local production of rail coaches, metros, aircraft, waterway equipment, and so on.

The Indian infrastructure revival should also become cognizant of what is needed to attract foreign and domestic tourists and make India a tourism hub. Tourism can be a great job generator for Indians and would boost the economy; the hospitality, health care, security and other industries can flourish too with the upsurge of tourism.

Biodiversity

We have done very little to conserve our biodiversity and even more importantly to get sustainable commercial gains out of it. The Vision 2020 documents had dealt extensively with the use of coastal marine resources. Similarly, our herbal resources need to be mined and streamlined for high-value commerce as has been done by the South-East Asian countries.

Chemicals

The government and industries need to launch a Mission Chemistry on the basis of the Technology Vision 2020 documents; we have highlighted several action points in Chapter 8. Knowledge chemicals should be our focus to achieve world-class standards by 2020, and later become world leaders.

The Knowledge Economy

This is an area of great concern. While computing services in India are quite good now, this sector may soon face serious problems when trying to expand and reach all Indians. This is because of a serious import-dependence in computer hardware. All policy measures need to be focused so that by 2020 most of the major manufacturing is done within India, whether by foreign companies, joint ventures or Indian industries. This would be the first part of the catch-up strategy.

Another weakness for India is that it does not have any major proprietary system or application software which is used all over the world. As a second part of our catch-up strategy, we should aim to have at least ten Indian software products selling commercially by 2020. For that we should create an innovation ecosystem with venture capital support for innovative ideas to be commercialized globally.

The step after that would be to have great industries in multiple fields with the potential to grow as multinationals.

Waste Management

We should have a three-part action plan that will make the present state of affairs a thing of the past by the year 2020.

1. Total garbage disposal in all metros, cities and towns, leading to a garbage-free urban India.
2. Waste-water recycling and reuse in at least half of urban India and in the inflows to major rivers like the Ganga and Yamuna. We should build channels on both sides of the river to receive the incoming municipal and industrial waste into rivers, and collect the waste water for recycling at certain specific intervals and allow the flow of recycled water into the rivers. We should also attempt waste-water recycling in at least 30 per cent of the highly irrigated agricultural areas.
3. Turn at least 50 per cent of waste in most parts of India into useful products like manure, animal/bird feed or energy.

Health Care

1. The greatest catch-up mission in this area should be to make the Mobile Diagnostic Centres already

approved under NHRM work at 100 per cent capacity by 2020.

2. In addition, we should step up all vaccination programmes without complacency.
3. We must improve sanitation facilities in towns, slums and rural areas, a project that should be completed by 2020.
4. Finally, we must create awareness for healthy lifestyles and physical fitness programmes. Our demographic advantage is derived from our huge youthful population, on whose health the future of India rests.

Security

Compared to what is needed and what is being done in the developed countries and in countries like China in this area, India's security infrastructure and skilled human resources are minimal. A lot needs to be done to catch up with the rest of the world. The first step would be to shed our complacency. What we will need to strengthen security is an integrated effort and continual monitoring. The defence services, internal security and cyber security are all areas where we need to utilize current information and facilitate modernization.

Education

Our objective here is to provide greater diversity of content and more options to the learning population, so that we can be more inclusive and build a large educated, skilled workforce. To facilitate this:

1. All young and middle-aged Indians should be skilled in contemporary economic and social skills.
2. Broadband coverage needs to be enhanced and sped up to enable e-education.
3. We need to review our educational material to discourage conventional rote learning and enable a new knowledge- and skill-based learning approach.

Emerging Areas

The reader may well say, when there is so much to catch up on, why must we struggle with new emerging areas just now?

The fact is that these emerging areas are not exactly beyond the horizon, seen only by especially farsighted persons. They have been experimented on worldwide; some are being tried out at a pilot level or an early commercial scale. There are several patents already on most of the technologies. If we wait for too long, catching up in these emerging areas will become that much more difficult.

We are only going to list a few emerging areas; the reason for this is that we did not find enough well-researched reports or a road map with an action plan for India that applies to the next twenty to twenty-five years.

In the course of our research, we did however come across such a report for China.[1] As we had mentioned in *India 2020*, China had also done its Vision 2020 exercise as its document then available had shown. It was very elaborate and had detailed road maps with possible targets for every five years.

The current China 2050 document is equally detailed. The premise of the document is that 'China must be fully prepared for an impending S&T Revolution' and it lists the new demands on S&T innovation in China's modernization process. The emphasis is on operational or commercial delivery for the final end uses or end users. For each item specific targets are set for the years 2020, 2030 and 2050.

While India's needs are different from China's, especially because of the differences in the sizes of the economies as well as governance systems, there are many important similarities between the two in terms of technological needs, be it for agriculture or energy. There are also a number of documents from the USA, especially the National Academy of Science and the National Academy of Engineering that cover a vast span of technologies and future commercial opportunities, some of which are relevant to India.

Against this background we would like to list a few emerging technologies which would be relevant for India, to make it globally competitive and to enable all Indians to have a better life and a future to look forward to. Some of these areas are:

- Biotechnological applications to agriculture, various GM crops to improve water stress resistance, increase the protein content of pulses and vegetables, insect resistance, etc.
- Climate change resistant agricultural methods: plant varieties, agronomic practices, etc.
- Soil biology application to improve degraded or degrading lands.
- Biotechnology and other biological practices to accelerate the growth of forests.
- Increase of biomass to provide a better source of renewable energy.

- Better animal varieties through the use of traditional artificial insemination and genetic engineering practices.
- Improving productivity of inland water fishes.
- Protection of biodiversity especially to save the endangered or nearly extinct plants, animals, birds, insects, etc.
- Shale gas exploration and study of its being a useful mix for Indian energy.
- Protection of coastal regions from the vagaries of cyclones, tsunamis and possible effects of climate change.
- Many chemical industry areas listed as emerging in the TIFAC reports quoted in Chapter 8.
- Bioprocessing and bioproducts.
- Revival of ground water resources.
- Use of coal in clean forms and methods for using the emissions as a regenerative part of the earth's ecosystem.
- Various new applications of nanotechnology in the Indian context.
- New cost-effective applications of space-based systems (coupled with ground systems) to provide communication reports for all Indians.
- Simple computer translations systems from Indian

languages to English and vice versa and from Indian languages to other world languages.

- Mining of Indian traditional knowledge bases for other applications.
- Various waste minimization techniques of manufacturing.
- Low-cost solar photovoltaic and solar thermal systems.
- Low-cost access to space.
- Space debris removal systems.
- Increasing safety and security of maritime cargo of Indian vessels.
- Various low-cost geriatric devices.
- Low-cost exercising tools for young, middle-aged and elderly Indians for better fitness.
- Low-cost housing without the use of large tracts of land in urban areas.
- Cyber-based training for upgrading the knowledge and skills of doctors and paramedics who work in the smaller towns and villages so that they can treat patients with confidence.
- Similar training for the 5000-odd skill sets required for the modern workforce (in areas like carpentry, plumbing, cooking, hairdressing, construction, etc.).

- Devices to increase the feeling of personal safety and security of ordinary citizens.

We would urge that Indian scientists, engineers, academics, businesspersons, policymakers and thought leaders, including those in the political field, should come together to arrive at a select, focused list of areas that will be particularly relevant to India in the future. That would be the first step to building our very own future India road map with a specified time target, not exceeding a decade.

15   Can India Do It?

In the Afterword to *India 2020*, we had said:

> India is a nation of a billion people. A nation's progress
> depends upon how its people think. It is thoughts
> which are transformed into actions. India has to think
> as a nation of a billion people. Let the young minds
> blossom—full of thoughts, the thoughts of prosperity.

This was written in 1998; sixteen years have passed
since then. India is now a country of 1.27 billion people
and still growing in population. As per the projections
in *India 2020*, India should have been much more
prosperous than what it is today. In reality, the bulk of
India is yet to see prosperity. Children born in 1998,
who will be sixteen now, see an uncertain future ahead
of them. They are not in a position to proclaim that

in six years' time, in the year 2020, they will be the proud citizens of a developed nation. India remains a developing nation, an emerging economy.

In the first chapter of *India 2020*, Dr Kalam had in fact outlined a second vision after that of national prosperity; it was a vision for a developed India. This is what he had said:

> [I]ndia has stood too long in the line of developing nations. *Let us, collectively, set the second national vision of Developed India.* I am confident that it is very much possible and can materialize in 15–20 years' time.

In 2018, four years from now, it will be twenty years since *India 2020* was written. The dream of becoming a developed nation has sadly remained just that, only a dream.

When we wrote *India 2020*, our vision, of course, extended to development beyond the year 2020. This was the way forward that we had charted:

Beyond 2020
The attainment of a developed status by 2020 does not mean that we can then rest on our laurels. It is an endless pursuit of well-being for all our people. Our vision of a developed nation integrates this

element of time within it as well. Only people with many embodied skills and knowledge and with ignited minds can be ready for such a long-term vision. We believe that it is possible to develop our people to reach such a state, provided we can follow a steady path and make available to the people the benefits of change all through their lives. They should see their lives and those of others improving in actual terms, and not merely in statistical tables.

Actions

This means the vision should become a part of the nation, transcending governments—the present and the future. To make this happen, several actions are required. An important element of these efforts is to develop various endogenous technological strengths. After all, technologies are primarily manifestations of human experience and knowledge and thus are capable of further creative development, under enabling environments.

Where Are We Today?

It is necessary to take a hard look at exactly where we stand in the world in terms of GDP. These are the latest (2014) figures.

TABLE 15.1 GDP of the Top
Countries in 2014
(in US$ billion)

1.	USA	17,528
2.	China	10,028
3.	Japan	4846
4.	Germany	3876
5.	France	2886
6.	UK	2828
7.	Brazil	2216
8.	Italy	2171
9.	Russia	2092
10.	India	1996

Source: knoema.com

The reader may wonder why such advanced countries like Germany, France, UK and Italy are lower than China on the GDP list. What we need to remember is that GDP is the sum total of production by all the people of a country. In an advanced country, though the productivity of people is very high, the number of those who produce is lower than in a developing country. For example, China has about four times the population of the USA and about ten times that of Japan. This is a demographic advantage that China has used very well. India has the same demographic advantage, but we have not skilled and developed our workforce sufficiently and also failed to develop local industries—which is why we are lagging behind in the tenth position.

Instead of just looking at the GDP figures we should look at GDP per capita as well. That is an indicator of how much a country has empowered its people in terms of their ability to produce high-value goods, how much wealth the individual citizen of a country creates—which of course depends on the work environment, the technologies a person is equipped with, his/her knowledge and skills, etc. (For example, a farmer using a tractor and having a good irrigation system at his disposal will obviously create more wealth compared to a person working in a dry land with a pair of bullocks and a plough.) The GDP per capita standings are the true indicator of how much India has been able to empower its citizens. These are some of the world rankings according to the latest (2014) figures.

This ranking makes it crystal clear how much progress we need to make to even be on par with China, Malaysia or Brazil. How do we raise the per capita GDP of the country? The answer is simple. We need to produce more, employing more of our

TABLE 15.2 GDP per capita Rankings in
2014 (calculated in US$)

Rank	Country
1	Luxembourg
2	Norway
5	Switzerland
6	Australia
9	Singapore
10	USA
18	Germany
19	France
21	UK
23	Japan
26	Italy
28	South Korea
61	Brazil
66	Malaysia
83	China
122	Sri Lanka
140	India

Source: knoema.com

population as part of the workforce, and thus generate
more wealth for every member of the population. It is
important to remember that our very large imports do

not count as part of our GDP, whereas our exports do. We need to import less and export more.

In order to make this happen, we need decisive leadership that can unite the country in a common mission to put India on a fast growth path, to reach, say, the third rank after the USA and China in terms of GDP and the top 50 list in terms of per capita GDP in a couple of decades, by the year 2035. Going forward from there, we can aspire to reach even higher rankings by the year 2050. But it will not happen easily. We will need to sink our differences and work very hard on this common mission under a leadership that is truly committed to the progress of the nation.

The Goals

We would now like to pinpoint the goals that we think India should aim for, looking ahead to the year 2020 and beyond.

Goal 1

India's economic growth rate needs to increase to double-digit figures from 2016–17 onward. The goal should be to reach the third position in GDP terms in the world, after the USA and China, by 2022. The year 2022 will incidentally mark seventy-five years of India's independence; on 15 August, the prime minister should be able to proudly announce this achievement from the Red Fort.

This is not a very difficult goal and if we achieve this, we will see a transformed India. Many more Indians will be uplifted economically, and a large percentage of the youth will be skilled in modern economic and social skills. They will form part of a great global workforce, with some 20 million people in each age group. There will be a number of global-level business enterprises in India. At least ten new mega businesses will emerge from India, along with some 1000 new start-ups. Indian scientific and technological inventions will become relevant to domestic and global needs. Some scientists working in India will qualify to be considered for highly valued awards like the Nobel Prize. Alongside, Indian art, culture, media and entertainment will be sought after in many countries, as our economy would have become sizeable and many youths from diverse backgrounds would have entered these fields. Similarly, Indian sportspersons will become a force to reckon with in international events like the Olympic Games.

But even with all this progress, India will not rank very high in the world in terms of GDP per capita; we may hover around the eightieth position.

Goal 2

By 2030, or earlier if possible, India should aim to rank in the top fifty in the world in terms of GDP per capita, with an aim to reach the twenty-fifth rank. To reach these levels, it is not enough to focus on economic growth alone; several other diverse steps in the social sectors and creating India-innovated products will be vital steps to getting us there.

Goal 1 and Goal 2 are intricately linked. It is not as though we can focus on and complete the Goal 1 targets first and then begin work on the Goal 2 targets. The two targets must be worked on together; in fact, Goal 1 leads logically to Goal 2.

For instance, for Goal 1, the targets in the education sector for the youth should be:

- Forty per cent getting higher educational qualifications
- Twenty per cent being very highly skilled after 10+2 education levels
- Forty per cent being relevantly skilled and literate

The percentages in the third segment would decrease as those in the first two increase. Obviously, these targets need to be planned carefully, not just chasing the Gross Enrollment Ratios (GERs) alone. It is not just the quality but the *diversity* in education and skills which will transform India.

In addition to education, the industrial sector, consumption standards, health services, and so on, need constant retuning with the GDP per capita numbers in mind. Only when each Indian is elevated economically, the Indian GDP per capita will rise in the global rankings. It is also important to remember that currently senior citizens (those above sixty years of age) comprise about 7 to 8 per cent of the Indian population. As better nutrition, health services and health awareness reach large parts of the population, this figure is likely to increase to 15 per cent by 2030. This will need to be taken into account when calculating per capita GDP.

Goal 3

Closely linked to Goal 1 and 2 is a third goal: to make India terrorism-free by 2020. There is a general feeling that India is a soft target for terror strikes—whether external or internal. This needs to change. A zero tolerance for terrorism, leading to zero incidences of terrorism, is the only way forward if India is to achieve real economic and social growth. Terrorism fragments society and damages national confidence; this is an obstacle that we must remove from our path. The reality is that as India grows economically, it will become the target of more terrorist action, as prosperous nations are. The coming decade is also going to be one with a great deal of turmoil in our neighbouring countries and serious sectarian conflicts in the Middle East, all of which might have ramifications in India. Local conflicts might also intensify in some parts of India. The country has to be firm and united in the face of these threats, and take decisive action to root out terrorism. This is crucial for India to march forward.

Alongside terrorism, we also need to urgently address another trend that is threatening half of India's population, namely crimes against women. We need to eliminate this threat completely if we are to become a secure and equitable nation making rapid economic and social progress.

Goal 4

The three goals above lead to a fourth goal which is the most important of all: that of a harmonious India.

India's beauty is not just in its biodiversity. It has a host of other diversities—of religions, languages, traditions, cuisines, musical forms, folklore, even anthropology. What makes India unique perhaps is its diversity.

While globalization and market forces may sometimes threaten diversity, modern communication methods and technological advances can also help preserve and enhance diverse cultures.

Some forces, often politically motivated, seek to make the very strength of diversity a weakness for India, by trying to exploit it to create divisiveness within society.

Each and every one of us needs to work with complete commitment for a harmonious India. Our long historical, civilizational and cultural traditions show that perfect harmony is possible within our diversity. This is the only way forward to building a great nation for the future. We must make it our mission to achieve this harmony around 2020.

Actions for All

All of us have a role to play in achieving these goals. But we would like to list the leadership roles that some specific people need to play.

Panchayat leaders

We will start at the grass-roots level. Panchayat leaders have a lot to contribute to build the country from the ground up. First and foremost, they should demand from their state governments that a PURA environment be built up around their villages, with a focus on a cluster of fifty or so networked villages. Their aim should be to have:

(a) physical connectivity
(b) electronic (broadband) connectivity
(c) knowledge connectivity and
(d) economic connectivity.

The other project panchayat leaders can pursue is to maintain and enhance water bodies in their locality, and to ask for irrigation canals and drip irrigation facilities.

Members of the Legislative Assembly

Local MLAs may concentrate on the prosperity of their constituency. They should aim at bringing in job-providing industries and skill-imparting centres. The other thing to pursue is to have a Mobile Diagnostic Centre in their area.

Members of Parliament

MPs have a much larger area of operation. They need to work with district administrations to speed up sanctioned projects and to help PURA projects which the panchayats in their constituency aspire for. They also have an important role to play in helping orient government schemes towards the constituency's economic growth and the welfare of the people. In fact, each MP can work out his/her constituency gross domestic product (CGDP) and work to increase it.

District-Level Administrators

Their mission is to try to provide the best governance possible. They can evolve a governance index and keep trying to improve it.

State Ministers

Their aim should be to increase their state's GDP by 10 to 15 per cent and also monitor the state's GDP per capita.

Central Ministers

They have to work for all the four goals we mentioned, and they have all of India to monitor. They must try to help the activities which are slow to speed up, and should specially encourage those that are doing well. They should incentivize the best performances, and demonstrate the best practices for others. It is their responsibility to improve the confidence of Indians in themselves and in their country.

The Opposition in States and at the Centre

Their role is to ensure that the government does not slacken the growth momentum.

Regulatory/Oversight Bodies

They perform an important role by keeping a vigil on government actions. They should do so while always keeping Goals 1 and 2 in mind. It is essential for the regulatory bodies to be involved from the beginning in a programme and periodically inform the concerned authorities on what is going right and what may be going wrong.

The Judiciary

The legal system has a crucial role to play especially with respect to Goals 3 and 4. The judiciary should also do its best to support India's economic growth, keeping pace with the dreams and aspirations of today's Indians.

Media

The media in all forms helps keep India vibrantly democratic. It is the media's responsibility to keep a constant vigil against wrongdoing; but it must also spread a positive message when there is good news to report.

The Corporate Sector

Our corporates are the engines of the economy. They need to be not only profitable and competitive in the domestic and world markets, but also have strong indigenous technological strengths. Indian industries (SMEs included) should aim at making India-designed, India-innovated, India-manufactured products and services reach all over the world.

Academic and S&T Institutions

While for a few years India will still be a follower economy, for it to achieve the third rank in the world in terms of GDP by 2022 will require original thought and innovative ideas. These need to come from our academia and scientific institutions. They need to change and adapt rapidly to the task at hand and align themselves to Goals 1 and 2.

Students and Youth

All youth should become students in some way. Their goal should be to prepare themselves for the future India, which will unfold very soon if many of the ideas we have discussed in this book are adopted. If the youth are skilled, if they are disciplined, if they are creative, if they are healthy and physically fit, India will achieve all the four goals we have listed.

The mantra for the youth should be:

Learn well
Learn many skills
Continue to learn
Learn to learn.

It is also very important for all our youth, including women, to join the workforce and contribute to the nation's productivity.

Agriculturists

They have a great future to build. They should learn to shed the idea of poverty, stop asking for subsidies, and ask instead for liberation from the plethora of controls. They should ask for upgrading technologies in agriculture and for asset creation.

Opinion Makers, Activists and Intellectuals

These key influencers often feel their voices are not heard. But it is for them to ensure that India focuses on the four goals at hand, and that the country takes the right steps forward in transforming itself over the next two decades.

Senior Citizens

Their number is large, totaling about 100 million, which is higher than the population of many countries. Many of them are educated and skilled; they should engage themselves in helping and guiding the youth to create the better India that they themselves could not see.

Doctors and Other Health Professionals

They have an important role to play in reaching quality and affordable health services to all Indians. Each one has to find his/her own method to help in the best way they can.

The important thing to remember is that every Indian, every one of us has a role to play as we look to build an India beyond 2020.

The twenty-first century will be India's if we work hard with a constant commitment and endeavour to better ourselves and transform India into the country of our dreams.

Can we do it? As Monk Samarpan says, 'You are much more than what you think you are, and you can achieve much more than you are achieving now.'[1]

Yes, we can do it!

The Mission

This is our four-point action plan for the nation:

1. Making ample water available for both urban areas and the 600,000 villages of the country, and for irrigation. This is possible only by developing a national smart waterways grid, ensuring water availability during times of drought, and also managing water storage and distribution during flood time.

2. Creating an earning capacity for every family, particularly the middle class and people who are below the poverty line. This is about 150 million out of the 200 million families in the country. This is possible only by establishing 7000 PURA clusters through physical, electronic, knowledge and finally economic connectivity.

3. Working towards achieving sustainable economic prosperity of the nation with the generation of employment potential for India's 600 million youth.

4. Evolving great citizens of India—this means that every citizen should have not only an earning capacity or the capacity to acquire knowledge but they should also become good human beings possessing great values. 'Where there is righteousness in the heart, there is beauty in the character.' This righteousness starts at home with the teachings of the mother and father and with one's first teachers.

Acknowledgements

We thank Penguin Books India for taking up this special book project. We would also like to place on record our sincere appreciation and thanks for the extraordinary editorial support extended by Udayan Mitra of Penguin.

Y.S. Rajan would like to add:

My sincere gratitude to Dr K. Radhakrishnan, chairman, ISRO, secretary, DoS, and chairman, Space Commission, for providing me with the facilities and ambience to continue my studies and researches in social, economic, technological and business issues of global and national importance. I am also grateful to Dr N. Mahalingam, founder editor, *Kisan World*, for giving me an opportunity to contribute a regular monthly column on such issues for about four years now; that has sharpened my thinking. My special thanks to my son Dr Vikram Rajan who had been an intellectual companion, critiquing and advising me on many philosophical and practical issues facing India and the world. Special thanks to S. Biswas, adviser DST/TIFAC, and his colleagues, whose TIFAC reports on chemicals and bio-products have been very useful. My loving thanks to my wife, Goma, our first son, Vijay, my daughter-in-law Mahalaxmi, aka Anu, and my grandsons Aditya and Ashwin whose love and affection sustain me. My thanks to Shailaja Krishnamurthy, my personal secretary, for taking care of many routine office matters, thus giving me more time for my creative pursuits. Thanks also to Smt. Ashalatha Laxminarasaiah, head, library and documentation, at the ISRO headquarters, who has ably provided me support in information searches. Last but not the least, I thank the many thousands of writers of papers, articles, reports, reviews and books including contributors to Wikipedia, who continue to enrich my knowledge and deepen my understanding.

Notes

Introduction

1. A.P.J. Abdul Kalam and Srijan Pal Singh, Target 3 Billion: PURA: Innovative Solutions towards Sustainable Development (New Delhi: Penguin Books, 2011).

Chapter 1: India @ 2014

1. http:/www.indianbusiness.nic.in/industryinfrastructure/ industrial%20sectors/food-process.htm. When the European Union is taken as a whole, India becomes second in the world in milk production.

Chapter 2: Learning from Missed Opportunities

1. Surabhi Agarwal, 'Why the Chips May Be Down for India's Fab Units', *Business Standard*, 12 November 2013.

2. Ibid.

3. Sourced from *Modern Manufacturing in India*, March 2013, pp. 20–21.

4. *Stage Non-Manufacturing: Governance and Policy Slack*, Iris Knowledge Foundation, Mumbai, with Forum for Global Knowledge Sharing, 2014.

5. Ibid.

6. Ibid, article by Aradhana Agarwal.

7. *Indian Express*, 26 August 2013.

8. Ibid.

9. Arvind Subramaniam, 'Underperforming Even in Good Times', *Business Standard*, 22 May 2013.

Chapter 3: Accelerating Agricultural Growth

1. 'The Indian Agriculture Sector: Investments, Growth and Prospects', January 2013, Indian Brand Equity Foundation (IBEF), www.ibef.org.

2. 'Global Review of Commercialized Transgenic Crops', *Current Science*, Vol. 84, No. 3, 10 February 2003.

3. 'GM Crops: A Story in Numbers', *Nature*, http://www.nature.com/news/specials/gmcrops/index.html.

4. Matin Qaim and Shahzad Kouser, 'Genetically Modified Crops and Food Security', *PLOS ONE*, 5 June 2013, http://www.plosone.org/article/info%3Adoi%2F10.1371%2Fjournal.pone.0064879.

5. David Zilberman, 'Genetic Edge', *The Hindu Business Line*, 26 March 2014.
6. Ashok Gulati, 'Against the Dole Model', *Times of India*, 24 April 2014.

Chapter 4: Manufacturing: Mega Possibilities

1. 'Economy of India', http://en.wikipedia.org/w/index.php?=606365315.
2. 'Indian Manufacturing Going Global', IBEF Report, November 2013.
3. Ibid.
4. World Bank Country Report: India, 2008.

Chapter 5: Mining: Adding Value to Our Natural Resources

1. From Wikipedia.
2. Ernst & Young Report on Mining, http://www.ey.com/in/industry/Mining.
3. D.R. Khullar, *Mineral Resources: India: A Comprehensive Geography* (Kalyani Publishers, 2006), cited on Wikipedia.

Chapter 6: Infrastructure: The Blood, Bones and Muscles of the Economy

1. IBEF Report, March 2014.

2. ICRA Research Services, June 2013, www.icra.in.
3. IBEF, Railways, March 2014.
4. IBEF, March 2014.

Chapter 7: Biodiversity: Balancing Commerce and Conservation

1. From Wikipedia.
2. Environment Audit Report, No. 17 of 2010–12, Chapter 3.
3. Ibid.

Chapter 8: The Chemistry of Life

1. 'Study on Indian Chemicals Industry, Technology Imperatives and Business Opportunities for Basic Chemicals', TIFAC-ICC Report, January 2014, www.tifac.org.in.
2. At the time *India 2020* was published.
3. 'Study on Indian Chemicals Industry, Technology Imperatives and Business Opportunities for Knowledge Chemicals', TIFAC-ICC Report, 2014, www.tifac.org.in.
4. 'Study on Indian Chemicals Industry, Technology Imperatives and Business Opportunities for Specialty Chemicals', TIFAC-ICC Report, 2014, www.tifac.org.in.
5. When Dr Kalam was principal scientific adviser (PSA) to the Government of India and Y.S. Rajan the scientific

secretary in 2000–01, one of our first tasks was to create a detailed action plan for herbal products through a task force. Sadly, the going has been slow since then.

6. Again, the Centre of Relevance and Excellence (CORE), the scheme specially launched by Dr Kalam as PSA and chairman, TIFAC, slowed down after he and Rajan left. We can easily convert about 200 colleges in India for this work, with low investment, and create skilled human resources in the process.

Chapter 9: The Neural Networks of the Knowledge Economy

1. IBEF Report on Telecommunication, March 2014, www. ibef.org.
2. While looking at this data we should remember that the rural population is almost twice the size of the urban population.
3. *The Hindu Business Line*, 20 June 2014.
4. 'Telecom: Enabling Growth and Serving Masses', Deloitte and CII, TeleTech 2014, www.deloitte.com/in.

Chapter 10: From Waste to Wealth

1. Asok Kumar Das, 'Solid Waste Management in India, Current Scenario'. Das is vice chairman, Indian Institute

of Chemical Engineers and the report is in the form of a Powerpoint presentation.

2. 'Process Intensification (PI) Technologies: Emerging Tool for Efficient Manufacturing' in 'Study on Indian Chemicals Industry, Technology Imperatives and Business Opportunities for Specialty Chemicals', 2014, www.tifac. org.in.

Chapter 11: Health Care for All

1. The age was 67.3 years for males and 69.6 years for females, figures for 2011–15, Ministry of Health and Family Welfare, Government of India.

2. The organized workforce comprises only 6 per cent of all Indians who are employed.

3. *Times of India*, 29 June 2014.

Chapter 13: Education for Every Indian

1. Y.S. Rajan, *Way Beyond the Three Rs: India's Education Challenge in the Twenty-First Century* (New Delhi: Penguin Books, 2010).

Chapter 14: Emerging Technologies: Catching Up and Forging Forward

1. *Science and Technology in China: A Road Map to 2050,*

editor-in-chief Yongxiang Lu, Chinese Academy of Sciences (Beijing: Science Press, and Springer, 2010).

Chapter 15: Can India Do It?

1. Samarpan, *Tiya: A Parrot's Journey Home* (New Delhi: HarperCollins, 2009).

About the Authors

A.P.J. Abdul Kalam (1931–2015) was one of India's most distinguished scientists. He was responsible for the development of India's first satellite launch vehicle, the SLV-3, and the development and operationalization of strategic missiles. As chairman of the Technology Information, Forecasting and Assessment Council, he pioneered India Vision 2020, a road map for transforming India into an economically developed nation by 2020, focusing on PURA (Provision of Urban Amenities in Rural Areas) as a development system for countrywide implementation.

Kalam held various positions in the Indian Space Research Organisation and the Defence Research and Development Organisation and became principal scientific adviser to the Government of India, holding the rank of a cabinet minister.

The President of India between 2002 and 2007, Kalam was awarded honorary doctorates from thirty-eight universities and the country's three highest civilian honours—Padma Bhushan (1981), Padma Vibhushan (1990) and Bharat Ratna (1997).

Kalam authored fifteen books on a variety of topics that have been translated into many languages across the world. His most significant works are *Wings of Fire, India 2020: A Vision for the New Millennium, Target 3 Billion* and *Beyond 2020: A Vision for Tomorrow's India.*

Yagnaswami Sundara Rajan is a well-recognized authority and a thought leader on technology development, business management and society linkages. He held various positions of responsibility related to science and technology between 1988 and 2002, and has shaped key policies and implemented several successful R&D projects with industry participation. He was responsible for creating a series of documents related to Technology Vision 2020. After a thirty-year stint with the government, he joined the Confederation of Indian Industry in 1996, where he was principal adviser from 2004 to 2010.

Currently an honorary distinguished professor at the department of space at ISRO, Bangalore and chairman at the Board of Governors at NIT, Manipur, he was awarded the Padma Shri in 2012.

Index

Index

solid waste management (SWM), 160–64

South Korea, 213

space debris removal systems, 238

space technology, 101, 237

special economic zones (SEZs), 121

special electronics exports zones (SEEZs), 226

speciality chemicals. *See* chemical industry

Sreedharan, E., 66, 103

steel. *See* iron ore and steel

strategic sector, 6

Subramaniam, C., 42

subsistence-wage service provider, 36

sugar industry, 63

Tata Institute of Fundamental Research (TIFR), 24

tax laws, 71, 73

tax reforms, 216

technology, technologies, 16–21, 212–39; technological development, 185, 188; enhanced education, 207; explosion, 142; road map, 134–36

Technology Vision for India 2020 (TVI 2020), 4–6, 49, 95, 142, 177, 213, 230

Technology, Information, Forecasting and Assessment Council (TIFAC) 4, 118–19, 134, 142, 164, 165, 177, 178, 179, 237. *See also* Indian Chemical Council (ICC)

telecommunication sector, 142, 145, 226

teledensity, 145, 147, 149

tele-education, 172, 207

telephone sector, 141

television channels, growth, 18, 143

terrorist attacks: security risk, 187–89; zero tolerance against, 189, 249–50

Texas Instrument, 26

textiles, 63–64, 66, 76, 117, 135, 225, 226

trade barriers, 124

training, relearning and reskilling, 134

transport sector, 157

unemployment, 27, 40, 209

United Nations (UN), 15

United States of America, 42, 52, 70, 125, 143, 165, 188, 192; 9/11 attacks, 189; freights, 103; GDP, 14; health care, 174; National Academy of Engineering, 236; National Academy of Science, 236; outsourcing of projects to India, 27–28, 30; pharma market, 126; population, 11; waste generation, 151, 152; waste management, 154

unorganized sector, 34, 36

uranium-based fuels, 156

urbanization, 94

waste: generation, 151–52; management, 117, 232; creation of wealth from, 151–65; recovery,

Index